HIDDEN AMAZON

The Greatest Voyage in Natural History

Dick Lutz

DIMI PRESS

Salem, Oregon

DIMI PRESS
3820 Oak Hollow Lane, SE
Salem, OR 97302-4774
©1999 by Dick Lutz

Printed in the United States of America

First edition, first printing

Library of Congress Cataloging in Publication Data:
    Lutz, Richard L., 1929-
        Hidden Amazon : the greatest voyage in natural
        history / Dick Lutz.
            p.   cm.
        Includes bibliographical references and index
        ISBN 0-931625-33-5 (pbk. : alk. paper)
        1. Natural history--Amazon River. 2. Natural history--Peru.
    3. Ecotourism--Amazon River. 4. Amazon River--history.
    5. Amazon River--Environmental conditions.   I. Title.
    QH112.L88   1998
    508.85'44--dc21   98-18054
                                                           CIP

*Quotations from Edward O. Wilson are reprinted by permission of the
publisher from THE DIVERSITY OF LIFE by E.O.Wilson, Cambridge, Mass.: Harvard University Press, ©1992 by Edward O.
Wilson.*

*Graphics from Princeton University Press by Andrea S. LeJeune are
used with permission.*

Cover design by Bruce DeRoos
Edited by Sue Henry, J. Marie Lutz
Typeface-12 pt. Palatino

"The forest of the Amazons is not merely trees and shrubs. It is not land. It is another element. Its inhabitants are arborean; they have been fashioned for life in that medium as fishes to the sea and birds to the air. Its green apparition is persistent, as the sky is and the ocean."

Henry Tomlinson

PREVIOUS BOOKS BY THIS AUTHOR

Feel Better! Live Longer! Relax. Salem, Oregon: DIMI PRESS, 1988.

The Running Indians (co-authored with Mary Lutz). Salem, Oregon: DIMI PRESS, 1989.

Komodo, The Living Dragon (co-authored with J. Marie Lutz). Salem, Oregon: DIMI PRESS, 1991.

Komodo, The Living Dragon, Revised Edition (co-authored with J. Marie Lutz). Salem, Oregon: DIMI PRESS, 1997.

To Mary

my wife, my friend, and my photographer

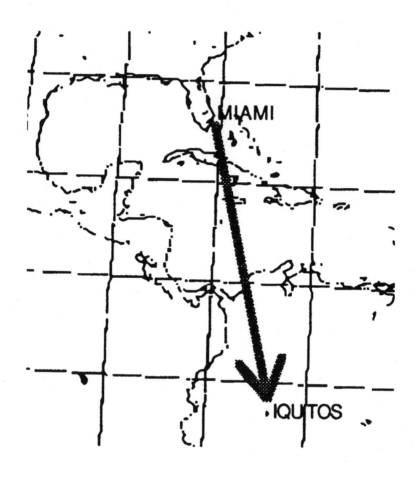

Miami to Iquitos is only about a four-hour flight.

ACKNOWLEDGEMENTS

Most of all, I'd like to thank the six people who read the galley of the book and gave me detailed comments on the contents. HIDDEN AMAZON is a better book due to their efforts. **Katie Brown** and **Veronica Rhoads,** International Expeditions; Roger Mustalish, President of the Amazon Center for Environmental Education and Research; **Peter Jenson,** Owner, Explorama Tours of Iquitos, Peru; **Ken Yagura,** friend and fellow world-traveler; and **Katherine White,** a Willamette University student.

Katie Brown not only gave me many corrections, she also suggested the title, arranged for me to use the artwork from International Expeditions, and encouraged me in my work.

Specific problems were solved by **Buzz Peavy** and **Russ Grimes,** International Expeditions; **Jaime Acevedo,** CONOPAC; **Nalini M. Nadkarni,** President, International Canopy Network; **Dr. James Duke; Alan Stanchfield; Dr. Harry Chinchinian; Ms. Debra Hitson-Ositis; Mike Schrunk;** and **Tom Holt.**

Tom Grasse, Dr. Richard Ryel, and all the staff at International Expeditions were helpful as were the crew of La Turmalina and the staffs of Explorama Lodge, Explornapo Camp, and ACEER. Of particular value were the three guides **Alfredo Chavez, Reni Coquinez,** and **Aristides Arevalo.**

The research could not have been done without the aid of the **Salem Public Library** (I'd like to particularly thank **Norma Johnson**), the **University of Washington Library,** and the **Greater Victoria (Canada) Public Library.**

Finally, thanks to my friends who traveled with me to the Amazon.

LIST OF ILLUSTRATIONS

Color:

Black & white:

AUTHOR'S PREFACE

This book describes the Peruvian Amazon. Using as a vehicle a trip on The Greatest Voyage in Natural History, a riverboat trip up the Amazon from Iquitos, Peru. Also included is the land expedition to the awe-inspiring Canopy Walkway. Two trips; one incredible, almost unbelievable experience.

In the seasonless tropics of the Amazon, the trips—one by river, one by land—are available at any time of the year. In this once-in-a-lifetime experience, you will not only have an enjoyable vacation while gaining a first-hand understanding of the tropical rainforest; you will also contribute in a very real way to the health and well-being of the residents in this third-world region. Even more important, your participation in these adventurous but comfortable trips will help the study and preservation of the magnificent Amazon Rain Forest.

This book is written not only for the armchair traveler, but also for the *doer*—the person who wants to experience something different and exciting, while at the same time contributing to mankind.

The Bibliography is annotated with comments about the material included. This will help you find further information should you be interested in knowing more. Whether you want to learn about the terrible explorer Aguirre or find detailed information about the birds of the Amazon, the Bibliography will direct you.

The many facts in this book were obtained either from direct experience or from authoritative sources. Though the facts were checked by the experts at International Expeditions and others, the final responsibility for the accuracy of this book remains with the author.

A portion of the profits from the sale of this book will be donated to the Amazon Center for Environmental Education and Research.

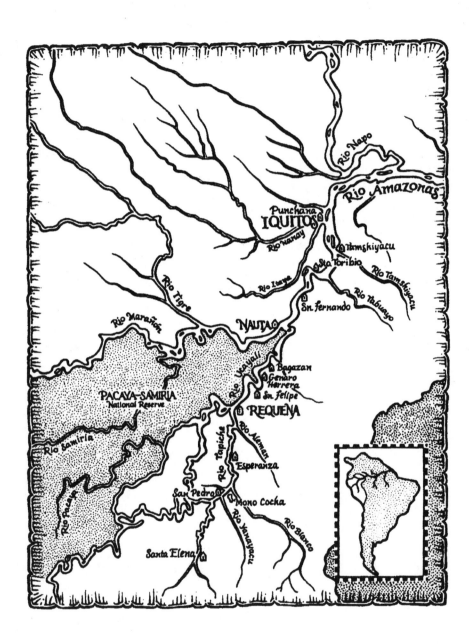

CONTENTS

International Expeditions by Hugh Hunter, Jr.

INTRODUCTION

The Amazon dazzles with its vastness and biodiversity. As you sail the wide, wide river you pass through a corridor of never-ending green, scores of variegated shades of green, like an artist's pallet. In the Peruvian Amazon are some 800 varieties of trees, but seldom do you see them clustered in same-species stands. Elsewhere in the world trees grow together—a stand of fir, a grove of elms or cottonwoods; but in the Peruvian Amazon the forest is like an ecumenical gathering of random individuals. Botanists believe there are a hundred thousand plant species in the entire Amazon region, including 30,000 kinds of flowers and 25,000 varieties of trees. And along with all that lushness, insects: two million species of them!

The river is the home of over 2400 species of fish, more than occupy the entire Atlantic Ocean. There are more than 4,000 species of butterflies and 1170 types of birds.

The Amazon Basin is wondrous in its sheer magnitude, and its superlatives. It is the world's largest drainage basin. Its 2.7 million sq. miles (7 million sq. km) drains 40 percent of the continent of South America and constitutes almost 5 percent of the total land area of Earth.

The Amazon River is both the longest and largest. It is 4200 miles (6720 km) in length. The Nile was called the longest until 1994, when a Peruvian research team headed by Loren McIntyre determined the Amazon's source was the Ucayali River, not the shorter Marañon as was previously charted. It has

"...the Amazon is a very special place, indeed the greatest celebration of the ecology of life that the planet has ever known."

Michael Goulding

1100 tributaries, 17 of them more than a thousand miles (1600 km) long. The river and its tributaries carry one-fifth of the fresh water in the world, more water than the combined flow of the next eight largest rivers in the world. The flow from its mouth is 2,829 million gallons (10,750 million liters) *per second*— five times the volume of the Congo and 12 times that of the Mississippi. It is 200 miles (320 km) at its mouth and no bridge crosses it for 3900 miles of its four-thousand-mile length. The "River Sea" and its tributaries carry an estimated 50,000 miles (80,000 km) of navigable waterways.

Although the earth's tropical moist forests (including those in Africa, Asia, Latin America, and the islands) represent only six percent of its land area, they contain about half the world's plant and animal species and produce 32 percent of the living matter on land.

This remarkable biodiversity is one of the reasons that the preservation of the rain forest is so important to all earth's life. And there is an urgency to the preservation because many of those tropical species are extremely vulnerable. Most are localized and exist nowhere else.

It is fashionable in some quarters to wave aside the small and obscure, the bugs and weeds, forgetting that an obscure moth from Latin America saved Australia's pasture land from overgrowth by cactus; that the rosy periwinkle provided the cure for Hodgkin's disease and childhood lymphocytic leukemia; that the bark of the Pacific yew offers hope for victims of ovarian and breast cancer; that a chemical from the saliva of leeches dissolves blood clots during surgery; and so on down a roster already grown long and illustrious despite the limited research addressed to it.

Edward O. Wilson, *The Diversity of Life*

It would be difficult to overstate how critically important it is to preserve the rain forests—or to reinvigorate our efforts. This book will show you how you can make a significant contribution to this effort while, at the same time, you learn more about the earth, broaden your horizons, and have a wondrous experience.

The way you can aid in the effort to preserve the Amazon forest is: Go there.

But isn't this contradictory? Doesn't an influx of tourists ruin a wild and attractive place? Perhaps it does in some places in the world, but not in the Peruvian Amazon.

By traveling there you provide jobs for local people. Then they no longer need to cut trees or hunt wildlife. The residents of the Amazon do not engage in destructive activities because they want to destroy, but because they have no other means of making a living. The fact is, the economic development experts in Peru and Brazil are strong advocates of tourism as an industry. Tourism brings the people an economy that does not depend upon the diminishment of resources.

Your going there also provides financial support to scientists researching the incredible resources of the rain forest. The most remarkable example of that is the Canopy Walkway. This "top of the forest" platform is made to be used by travelers and scientists alike. The walkway is maintained by the non-profit Amazon Center for Environmental Education and Research (ACEER), in partnership with the Peruvian non-profit organization called Conservacion de la Naturaleza Amazonica del Peru (CONOPAC). These are but two of the many 'NGOs' (non-governmental organizations) that are working to save the rain forests.

The Upper Amazon has an intriguing geological history. The Ice Age transformed the Basin millions of years ago. As the original vegetation retreated westward toward the slopes of the Andes the area became a vast grassland. Isolated pockets of tropical lowland, however, became forested havens for the plants, animals, birds, and insects that adapted to the changing biome.

As the climate changed again and rain returned to the Basin, those pockets became centers from which species of flora and fauna radiated throughout the Amazon area.

Before the Andes Mountains were formed, the great river flowed from east to west, not eastward as it does today. When the mountains erupted about fifteen million years ago they dammed the river, creating a vast lake that covered much of the present-day Basin. Over geological time the lake waters worked eastward, forming the channel the Amazon now traverses. The result—the rain forest came into being.

Many aquatic mammals—dolphins and manatee, for example—apparently were ocean-dwellers that were trapped by the formation of the Andes. They adapted to the ecological change and their descendants now inhabit the fresh-water lakes of the Upper Amazon.

"This was wilderness in the sixteenth-century sense, as it must have formed in the minds of the Portuguese explorers, its interior still largely unexplored and filled with strange, myth-engendering plants and animals. ... And I thought: there is still time to see this land. ..."

Edward O. Wilson

The Upper Amazon lies in Peru. About half the river is within that nation's borders. Though the Basin occupies about 60 percent of Peru's area, only six percent of its twenty million people live there. Peru is an economically struggling nation doing what it can to preserve the rain forest.

The Amazon Basin is the earth's largest region to benefit so much and suffer so little from geological changes. Scientists have identified six major geological transformations:

1) The separation of the continents;
2) The appearance of flowering plants;
3) The rise of the Andes Mountains;
4) The reversal of the Amazon's course;
5) The temperature fluctuations of the Ice Age.
6) Civilization

The historical record shows that after each of those first five transformations, the number of plant and animal species in the Basin area increased.

The sixth transformation is underway today: The human encroachment into the area and the concurrent reduction of the diversity of living things. The commonly used descriptive is "destruction of the rain forest." Although this transformation by humans is the one resulting in decreased diversity, it impacts the Peruvian section of the Basin less than elsewhere. Despite the near extinction of a few animal species (primarily due to hunting), more plant and animal species exist in the Peruvian Amazon area than ever.

The region around Iquitos, Peru, is perhaps the wettest part of the Amazon Basin (over 100 inches of rainfall annually). It is also the most pristine.

The principal geography of the Basin is the huge river system; but a number of ox-bow lakes are scattered throughout. They are formed as the meandering river changes course, the left-over remains of channels which once were. They remain as crescent-shaped expanses of open water: ox-bows.

Like other rivers flowing through flat plains, the Amazon and its tributaries constantly change course. Throughout your river and land trips, your guides point out old channels, growing over with new vegetation.

The Peruvian Amazon—the Hidden Amazon—is the focus of this book. That this region is "hidden" is emphasized by the fact that virtually all books, articles, and other references deal mostly, even exclusively, with the Brazilian portion of the forest. Yet the river originates in Peru and 46 percent of its length is in that country.

Why the prevailing focus on the Brazilian Amazon, and why the neglect of the Peruvian portion?

The historical reason is that Brazil was settled by the Portuguese, who, in the sixteenth and seventeenth centuries exploited the resources. Their first exploitation was of the native Indian peoples, whom the Portuguese enslaved. The Portuguese stayed and, to this day, Portuguese is the language of Brazil. The Spaniards settled the rest of Central and South America; but as soon as they determined there was no gold in the upper Amazon, they left. The Brazilian Amazon was already claimed and the Peruvian Amazon gave the Spanish no reason to stay.

The geographical reason is that Peru is 2500 miles (4000 km) upriver from the mouth;

and before air travel came into its own, the only way to get there was by river. It was a long and perilous voyage. To take that much risk there had to be a *lot* of gold ... and there wasn't any. To further make the area inaccessible, the Andes Mountains west of the river form an almost untraversable barrier between the coast and the river basin. Even today, transportation by land is nigh impossible so the fact that the Peruvian rain forest has been kept hidden is entirely unsurprising. In some ways, that isolation has benefited the region.

In Brazil, the construction of roads, of government-sponsored colonization projects, and large-scale mining and hydroelectric plants destroyed a significant portion of the natural environment. The city of Manaus has been polluted by large-scale burning of the surrounding rain forest. But Manaus is a thousand miles (1600 km) from Iquitos, Peru, and the region around Iquitos remains relatively clean.

In recent years some oil has been extracted from the Peruvian forest, but in amounts so small it has had minimal ecological effect on the jungle. However, the oil companies continue to salivate over the immense resources they believe the Amazon Basin holds. Peru, the poorest nation in South America, is under constant pressure to fill its empty coffers by granting permits to explore for oil in the jungle. The major region under consideration is west of our part of the forest.

Compared to rain forests elsewhere in the world, deforestation of the upper Basin is relatively slight; of all the Amazon subregions that area is among the least damaged. Thus, if you want to see virgin tropical rainforest, the Iquitos-based trips of International Expeditions would be your ticket. Iquitos is only four air hours from Miami.

This book specifically describes two areas of the great river known as the Amazon. Both are in Peru. One is the Ucayali-Marañon Rivers area upriver from Iquitos. The other is the Napo River area downriver from Iquitos towards the Brazilian border.

The riverboat *La Turmalina* is your vehicle for the Ucayali-Marañon trip, known as "The Greatest Voyage in Natural History." Embarking from Iquitos, it offers air conditioning, hot showers, roomy cabins, excellent food, and an attractively aesthetic decor. How remarkable that such splendor takes you to one of the most remote and wildlife-filled areas in the world!

The other trip, the journey into the Napo River area, takes you to the largest Canopy Walkway in the world.

A word about your comfort: The Greatest Voyage in Natural History, the river voyage, pays much more attention to the soft life. The land expedition, which offers rather primitive accommodations and occasional slogging through mud, is great for those who enjoy the mildly rigorous life.

Generally speaking, the travelers on the riverboat voyage are older than those on the land expedition. One of our companions on the land expedition had difficulty walking. She declined to go on the jungle walks but she was taken to the three camps by boat.

It would be difficult to overstate the importance of preserving the rain forests. This book will show you how you can contribute to the preservation of the Amazon forest—

while you learn more about the world, broaden your horizons, and have a wonderfully enjoyable vacation. It is a chronicle of Mary's and my journeys, and of how, we conscientiously believe, we contributed to the Amazon—and it to us.

The Amazon River

It flows from near the Pacific Ocean in the East
to the Atlantic Ocean. Its length is 4000 miles.

CHAPTER 1

ON THE RIVER

O *ur comfortable four-hour flight from Miami lands in Iquitos, Peru. The Iquitos airport has a musty smell, which I guess is the jungle. The airport displays many souvenirs and decorations representative of the jungle. Wooden butterflies, bows and arrows, and examples of Indian art are just some of the objects on the walls of this interesting building.*

*I was surprised. This was supposed to be an expedition into the wilds of the Amazon jungle; yet here we were, pillowed in cushy comfort. After the usual customs rigmarole, we were prepared to rough it on the Amazon. Instead, an air-conditioned bus took us to our air-conditioned boat. After introductions by our guides, we were assigned our spacious cabins on **La Turmalina** and since it was midnight by then sleep came easily.*

Forty percent of food crops grown in North America originated in Latin America. Some of our staples from the Amazon Basin are corn, potatoes, sweet potatoes, sugar cane, coffee, and tomatoes, plus rubber and

"Perhaps no country in the world contains such an amount of vegetable matter on its surface as the valley of the Amazon"

Alfred Russel Wallace

tobacco. Manioc, the dietary staple of Amazon residents, is native to the area as well.

Yet despite that influence, and despite the statistical superlatives of the area, the Amazon is, without a doubt, the least known major river in the world. The mystery of the Nile, on the other hand, was rather quickly unraveled after people traveled west from Zanzibar to Lake Victoria in 1862. The first immigrants landed in Australia in 1788, and within eighty years that continent had been quite thoroughly explored. Antarctica was first seen in 1829 and within a century man had visited the South Pole.

The Amazon, in contrast, was discovered over 450 years ago, about the same time Europeans arrived in North America; yet the Amazon still awaits exploration. The great river and its basin, particularly the Peruvian section that is our focus, remains much as it was in those early days of exploration.

In his book, *Explorers of the Amazon*, Anthony Smith says this:

> ... it is still possible to see the river as the early adventurers saw it. This is quite unlike standing on Manhattan and trying to visualize it from Peter Stuyvesant's viewpoint, or imagining Sydney Harbor when the first ships sailed in. On the Amazon there are sand banks, floating logs, toucans pushing their bills through the air, the sound of parrots and macaws, much as these things have always been. The trees still line river-banks, the Rio Negro is still black, and the caimans still stare as unblinkingly as when those first hungry boatloads of Spaniards could think of little else but food.

CHAPTER 2

THE MIGHTY AMAZON

We awoke to find ourselves sailing up the mighty Amazon River. *La Turmalina* had gotten underway while we slept.

First I peered out the window, then rushed out on deck, and viewed the awe-inspiring great Amazon River. Grandiosely wide it was, and fast-flowing. Later in the journey we shall challenge narrower streams; but here we felt both small and expansive. On either side of this vast waterway: walls of green, green clear to the curvature of the earth.

We occasionally saw small fields cleared by the local people. On these carved-out farms they have created sustainable local economies, raising bananas, manioc, and other crops, and growing livestock on pastureland.

Scores of logs, even whole trees, floated down the river, making me fear damage to the boat. Then I thought: No fear; *La Turmalina* is being skillfully steered by an experienced crew.

"Even the most highly trained botanists are humbled by the immense diversity of the Amazonian forests."

Wade Davis

The river drains an area about the size of the United States. The Amazonian rain forests create half their own rainfall, and no one yet knows how depletion of the forests may affect the physics of the water cycle. Rainfall here averages 100 inches (250 cm) a year. The temperature remains in the 75° to 80° F range (24° to 27° C) year-round; but the high humidity makes it feel hotter. Trees, though they are deciduous, are always green and fruits and flowers ripen and bloom the year around. The moist, warm air causes luxuriant growth of the dense rain forest even though the soil is not very fertile.

International Expeditions by Mason Fischer

Although other sections of the Amazon have definite rainy and dry seasons, the area around Iquitos really doesn't. Dr. Alwin Gentry studied the unbelievable biodiversity of the area. Among other approaches, he examined the reports of the Iquitos Airport which has kept excellent records of rainfall since the first days of World War II. Dr. Gentry found that any month of the year could be the heaviest rainfall month.

Despite the lack of a rainy season/dry season there are definite high water/low water periods. These are completely different from rainy or dry seasons as the water level is affected by more than just rain, e.g. the rate of evaporation of the flooded rain forest and the transpiration of plants. Rain falls, on the average over 200 days a year. Some locals may tell you that there is a rainy season and a dry season but Peter Jenson, a scientist who has lived in Iquitos over 30 years, says there is not.

The flooded forest is the spawning ground for many species of fish. It is a veritable feasting site for insect-eating fish, and an orchard. The Amazon is the only place in the world where many of the main foods of the fish are fruit and seeds. Scientists believe the fish locate their food by smelling the fruit as well as seeing it, and hearing it drop into the water.

Intermittently the shoreline is broken by *chacras*, small clearings inhabited by a family or two. Usually, when we passed by, a few family members were on the banks or on the river in dugout canoes.

The staple fruit cultivars here are bananas, plantains, and papaya, though there are others, too, and rice is an important crop. The local residents also utilize the many wild fruits.

In past times, dozens of Indian tribes lived in the area we traveled. Now, most of the tribes that still exist have moved into the jungle's interior where hunting is better.

Ribereños (river dwellers) are the mixed-blood residents of the Peruvian Amazon. Though ribereños do not consider themselves Indians, their ancestors were the aboriginal Indians and the people who later came to the area—from elsewhere in Peru, South America, or Europe. These immigrants most likely came during the rubber boom.

Although short on material possessions, the ribereños are cordial and gracious. They are also called "the invisible people," from having been given little notice by their national government or by anthropologists. While the Peruvian government has granted some Indian tribes exclusive rights to their traditional hunting and fishing grounds, the ribereños get no such protection. Commercial fishers plunder traditional ribereño fishing grounds in a waterway rights free-for-all.

Like all cultures, the Peruvian Indians have explained natural phenomena through belief in the supernatural. For instance, the historical record shows that at eight o'clock on the morning of August 13, 1930, one or more large meteorites fell in the jungle some 200 miles from Iquitos. Local oral history says the sun turned blood-red and darkness fell. A fine red dust sifted to the earth. Several loud whistles filled the air followed by three explosions, each shaking the ground with earthquake-like tremors.

A Catholic missionary, **Father Fedele d'Alviano**, came upon the nearby Indian village five days later. As he arrived the natives were all gathered together, about to ingest timpo, a neurotoxic poison. The priest arrived just in time to deter the people who, convinced that the world was about to end, were about to commit mass suicide.

Anthropologists tend to classify indigenous cultures as hunters, gatherers, or fishers. The ribereños, though, are all of these and more. They hunt, gather, and engage in agriculture, and they use a wide range of forest products for both subsistence and as added-value products of a cash economy. From the forest come their own home-building materials, medications, and clothing, as well as products they sell on the market.

Although they as a group do not speak the native dialects, worship animist gods, or don traditional garb for everyday wear, the ribereños have retained practices that have served Amazonian peoples so well for centuries. They still use traditional technologies and products for farming, hunting, fishing, and treating illnesses.

Many social scientists believe the inhabitants of the Amazon had the potential to become an advanced people, but several forces combined to thwart their development.

First, the Jesuit missionaries who arrived soon after Europeans "discovered" the area imposed severe discipline. It was partly an effort to stamp out the cannibalism occasionally practiced by the Amazonians, partly to convert them. The missionaries' rules were based upon western morals and mores and religion without regard to the native culture or ecology. The clergy abhorred that Europeans enslaved the Indians (and Indians made slaves of other Indians), insisting that Indians must be treated as humans, not as animals. However, the Jesuits made no attempt to educate, advance, or develop the people or their economy. It was as though the missionaries wanted to lead but not to allow local citizens to learn leadership. For instance,

"The nontribal, forgotten folks of the Amazon have no way of protecting the natural resources of forest and water that are the basis of their subsistence."

Christine Padoch

despite a shortage of Jesuit missionaries, no Indian ever became a Jesuit priest. The rigidity of the Jesuits stultified the Indians. The missionaries' sudden departure in the eighteenth century left the Indians leaderless and still uneducated and thus unable to further their own development, at least according to Industrial Revolution standards for "development."

Second, diseases unknown in the Western Hemisphere were introduced by the European explorers, missionaries, and settlers. Many Indians fell ill and succumbed, weakening the tribes.

Third, the rubber boom at the turn of the century resulted in near annihilation of the Indians, not too unlike the "opening of the West" in the United States, resulting in the same thing. There are no reliable statistics showing how many true Indians still reside in the Peruvian Amazon.

Nevertheless, anthropologist Betty J. Meggers concluded that environmental conditions were such that Amazonia could never have become a "cradle of higher civilization."

In his contribution to *Frontier Expansion in Amazonia*, Anthony Stocks writes of four "Indian policies" that have been pursued over centuries.

The first, which he calls "the civilization policy," was imposed mainly by missionaries who intended to transform the Indians into the Western culture.

The second, a "conquest policy," has been carried out by commercial interests, the military, political leaders, the church, and even the Indians themselves. Its goal is supposed to be "economic development and progress" (whatever that is). In the last analysis, conquest policy seems based on the belief that the land and its resources are more valuable than the people.

The third, which Stocks calls "advocacy," calls for assisting the Indians in assuming a place in the modern world while still protecting their rights to their traditional land and resources and preserving aspects of their culture they choose to retain. This may be viewed as a paternalistic approach, as in the case of reservations in the U.S. and reserves in Canada. Advocacy has been rare in Peru.

The fourth policy is "extermination"—disavowing native peoples' rights of certain privileges and protection by national government, and various attempts to assimilate them. Extermination has not been an official policy in Peru as much as it has been elsewhere in South America. Arguably, that has been the policy of practice of certain commercial interests. The most obvious example is the rubber boom along the Putumayo River.

In the 1970s Peru's estimated Indian population was 220,000, over twice the number of Indians in Brazil. This figure includes all of Peru, not simply the Amazon region. Part of the reason Peru's native population is greater is because at one time Peru was a refuge for Indians fleeing enslavement.

Following a military coup of the Peruvian government in 1968, the new government launched an effort to "solve the Indian problem." Largely it was a socialist plan: Build some villages, legalize rights to lands the Indians had occupied for centuries. The effort, mostly in an area west of where *La Turmalina* explores, came to little.

In the 1970s the pendulum swung, but this time, instead of rubber it was oil. The Peruvian government granted rights to oil companies to explore the area; but there were no major finds, a boom never happened, and most of the oilers departed. In the process, the forest was trampled; and diseases carried in by the explorers and drillers nearly wiped out several Indian villages. The Amazon and its people are fragile.

In the Amazon are many tribes, many languages, many varied cultures—too many to enumerate here. As an example, though, let a description of the Omagua represent all of the Indian tribes.

Omagua means flathead. In earlier times, the Omagua placed their small children's heads between boards and tied them so tightly the heads could not grow in width, only in length. An early Spanish explorer commented scornfully that the effect was "more like a poorly shaped bishop's miter than the head of a human being."

The Omaguas were said to be proud and talkative. And lazy. Reputedly, they were happiest when they were lying in their hammocks with slaves attending them. Yes, slaves—captives from other tribes. Their land evidently yielded a plentiful, easily gathered food supply.

This tribe of Indians originated several hundred miles below the Rio Napo, moving into the Marañon-Ucayali area in 1710, when they fled the Portuguese slave traders.

Before the aboriginal culture was essentially destroyed at the time of their move to the upper Amazon, early explorers and missionaries documented it well enough to lend insight into the ancestral culture of the present-day Omagua.

Most Omagua villages were situated on islands, beaches, or banks of the Amazon. At one time Omagua settlements formed an almost continuous line of houses for 200 leagues on the shores and islands of the Amazon. The records cite one village of 330 individuals in 28 houses. With an average of eleven-plus persons per household, one hopes the homes were large ... and they were. They were rectangular structures, with walls of cedar planks and roofs of thatched palm. Inside, the houses were kept cleanly swept (the Peruvian Indians have a reputation for cleanliness), and furnished with hammocks, large mats woven of palmleaf, and pottery vessels. Indian and ribereño homes today, at the turn of the millenium, are very much the same.

The men wore knee-length sleeveless cotton shirts called cushmas; women were clad in knee-length cotton skirts and sometimes a little mantle. The Omaguas painted their cloth in multi-colored designs.

Each household kept one or two servants who were captured in childhood from neighboring tribes. They were servants rather than laborers, and the record notes that the servants were not mistreated.

In their journals, the explorers and missionaries describe the Omagua as warriors. Constantly warring. They raided villages in the interior to get two things: revenge and slaves. After they captured a village the bloodthirsty Omagua immediately killed all the old people. Younger men and tribal leaders were put to death in ceremonial rituals, their heads taken home as trophies. The children of the defeated village were taken home as slaves. You may have read of the head-shrinking formerly done by the Peruvian Indians, but that was performed by the Jivaro tribe to the east.

For long voyages, warfare, and crop transportation, the Omagua made huge dugout canoes of cedar. The canoes were 45 feet (14 m) long.

In the 18th and 19th centuries, the Omagua were widely known for the numerous rubber articles they manufactured. These included water bottles.

The origin of the Omagua is not known for certain, but anthropologists use cultural traits as clues to peoples' roots. Many Omaguan practices, such the wearing of cotton clothing and the flattening of children's heads were characteristics of the ancient Incas. By 1976, there were only an estimated 600 Omaguas left.

Amazonian agriculture is very different from ours. Due to its frequent leaching by floods, most of the soil is extremely poor in nutrients. Where land is cleared and crops planted (principally the regional staple, manioc), the soil is exhausted in two years. Then it must lie fallow for fourteen to twenty years. Weeding is done by machete; the land is seldom tilled.

Slash-and-burn agriculture sounds destructive but it is actually efficient and productive in the forest—as long as it is sparsely populated. The burning of trees and forest-floor vegetation actually increases soil nutrients in the short term. However, there are fewer nutrients in soil which has been planted repeatedly than in undisturbed forest soil. After a patch of land is cleared and two or three crops have been grown on it, it is abandoned and allowed to return to its native state.

The trees harvested in largest quantities are mahogany, cedar, and certain types of rosewood. Mahogany wood is extremely valuable, but the trees are not particularly plentiful in the Amazon rain forest and their cutting is restricted. Cedar is widely used by the ribereños and Indians for their dugout canoes. Your guide will demonstrate the process of canoe making.

We lunched and napped, then transferred to a smaller boat for our first trip away from our main boat. Our 23-person group was divided into two tour groups, each in a boat led by one of the two guides. A La Turmalina crew member piloted each of the open, outboard motor-powered boats. The crew members were obviously of Indian descent, being short, dark, shy, and very helpful.

As we traveled up the main river we had seen egrets, parrots, and some other birds, but now, on the tributary, we saw many more. We also saw our first huge water lilies.

The giant Victoria Water Lily (*Victoria amazonica* or *victoria regia*) has enormous (several feet across) floating leaves which can support the weight of a small child. These remarkable plants bloom at sunset, then close as dark falls and the temperature drops. When the flowers are open, beetles are attracted by the bright whiteness, intense scent, and the heat generated within the flower. Then, as the flowers close, the beetles are trapped inside the petals. When the lilies open the next evening the beetles escape. Covered with pollen, the bugs traverse to another water lily and pollination occurs. The Amazonian version of the birds and the bees.

The water lily's flower is white only on its first blooming. The following evening, after the beetles have spent the night, the opening-up blossom is red or green. The beetles land only on the white flowers; thus, they are always in the right flower at the right time.

You will certainly see this plant at various places on both of the trips described in this book. *Victoria amazonica* is but one of many examples of the amazing synergy between plants and insects in the Amazonian rain forest.

Our group spotted a red-headed caiman iguana swimming in the river. A relatively rare creature, this one was about three feet (1 m) long.

Green iguanas, on the other hand, are seen regularly, usually in trees. They may be as long as 7 feet (2.2 m). Iguanas are harmless. In Panama, iguanas are raised commercially for food, which, it is said, taste much like chicken.

We also saw some dolphins on this day's excursion. It was to be the first of many times we would observe them. There are two varieties of fresh-water dolphins (river dolphins), one pink, the other gray. (Some writers claim they are the same variety, that the pink ones are older individuals.) They reach 6 to 7 feet (2 m) in length, have pink skin, tiny eyes, and a humped back.

There is not much difference between them, except that when they surface to breathe the grays leap clear of the water, while the pinks show only a portion of their back. Like their close relatives the whales, dolphins breathe through a blowhole on top of their head. The gray thrives equally well in salt water or fresh; the species is found in coastal South America and in Asia. The pink dolphin, in contrast, is no world traveler—it lives only in the fresh water of the Amazon and its tributaries.

Dolphins are relatively long-lived, with some individuals reaching age twenty or older. They do not begin to breed until five to eight years of age, possibly older. The female bears a single calf after a gestation period of eight to eleven months, depending on the species. The calf is born under water, then the mother immediately nudges it to the surface for its first breath of air. The young stay with their mothers for one to two years, while continuing to nurse.

International Expeditions by Buzz Peavy

River dolphins have smaller brains than their ocean-dwelling counterparts, and they are less socially interactive among themselves. River dolphins' eyes detect light but do not process images. Thus in their murky habitat they rely on their sonar abilities to find food (mostly fish and shrimp) and to avoid running into objects. Their sonar headquarters is located in the "melon" on the top of their heads, which contains their transmitter and part of their receiving system. The remainder of their receiving apparatus is in the jaw, which enables them to search beneath themselves and in all directions. The dolphins' sonar equips them to determine the size, direction, density, and speed of objects. The hairs covering their long snouts are also used as feelers to locate food.

These curious animals will most surely be seen on any Amazon trip. They are plentiful because they are seldom hunted by the local people.

Dolphins are feared by both the Indians and ribereños, because of the tradition that says the creatures can assume human form. For instance, if a woman becomes pregnant after a feast, she can claim that a dolphin transformed itself into a handsome man and seduced her. Although it is easy to assume that this is ancient Indian myth, scientists think that it is not so ancient at all. They believe the stories actually derive from river cultures that emerged after the European conquest of the region.

*Back on **La Turmalina** after our small-boat excursion, we came to the fork where the Ucayali and Marañon Rivers converge. It is at this point the waterway is geographically designated as the*

*Amazon, and that is the mighty river's name un-
til it reaches the Atlantic Ocean some 2600 miles
(4160 km) away. But its total distance-of-record
extends on up the Ucayali. That is where **La
Turmalina** goes.*

*It is the Ucayali River where sightings of phan-
tom boats (barcos fantasmas) have frequently been
reported. Sometimes they have been seen in the
swirling mists of early morning or evening, but
there have also been numerous sightings of boats
materializing and then disappearing in mid-day.
Entire village populations have seen these appari-
tions. Perhaps this is an area of mirages ... or perhaps . . . At any rate, keep your eyes open as you
sail the Ucayali!*

For some time, scientists have disputed
whether the Nile or the Amazon is the world's
longest river. In 1971 geographers pinpointed
the source of the Amazon and concluded that
it was longer. Yet that wasn't really definitive
because sections of the Amazon constantly
change channels. Another variable is that at
the mouth of the Amazon is an island that is
roughly the size of Switzerland. Whether the
true Amazon is in the North Channel or the
South Channel makes a couple of hundred
miles difference!

In the end, does it matter? The Nile and
the Amazon are both right around 4000 miles
(6400 km) long. But the Amazon carries five
times more volume of water.

*Our guides discussed the possibility of going
to visit a shaman this evening, but they discovered he was in the process of moving because the
river was rising near his home. In the end, we did
not make the visit.*

The shamans apply their rituals to heal, to lift curses (or to invoke them), and for other purposes. Though the rituals vary in detail, one common denominator is the use of hallucinogenic drugs derived from Amazonian plants. Numerous native plants contain substances which, when smoked or ingested, lead to mind-altering experiences. (For anyone interested in the details, I suggest Wade Davis's *One River*.)

There is a growing camaraderie among the 23 travelers. Several of the crew speak some English; they are interesting to talk with.

The dining room and the upper deck are gathering places for company and comfort. The air-conditioned dining room commands an exceptional view behind and on both sides of us. The food is uniformly excellent. Most of us gather on the upper deck for drinks before dinner and evening conversation after dinner. When you go there, be sure to sample the Pisco Sour, the Peruvian national drink. This delightful libation is made from grape brandy, egg white, lemon juice, and sugar syrup, whipped together and served with a dash of Angostura bitters. Delicious!

CHAPTER 3

THE RIO TAPICHE

During breakfast this morning we passed Requena, a town of about 10,000 located on the banks of the Ucayali. In the 1960s, some colonists from Requena invaded the home territory of a small Indian tribe known as the Matsés. Defending their territory, the Matsés retaliated against the invaders. The Peruvian army was sent in and, along with some vigilantes from Requena, attacked the natives. Using jet planes, helicopters, machine guns, and other modern weaponry (most of which the United States had previously provided to the Peruvian army), the army dispersed the natives. For seven years the surviving Matsés hid in the forests, until, in the early 1970s Protestant missionaries from the Wycliffe Bible Translators induced the natives into their first contact with others.

We saw a river bus anchored at Requena. The buses are boats, actually. These passenger vehicles, which come in varying degrees of comfort, are the favored method of transportation on the

Amazon, at least for those who want to travel further than their dugout canoes can carry them.

This river bus, our guide told us, was going to the city of Pucallpa, about 250 miles (400 km) from here. That is, if you measure the distance from point to point on a straight line on a map. But the Amazon does not flow in a straight line, so the trip on the winding river is probably twice that distance. The trip will take five days.

As we breakfasted that morning, two Peruvian navy ships passed us.

During our morning small-boat excursion we explored some minor tributaries. We watched some birds dive for fish. We saw a curious sight—five egrets standing in a row, still as sculptures. We also saw five water buffalo surrounded by a flock of egrets. The water buffalo were not wild animals but domesticated livestock belonging to some residents along the river. One occasionally sees other livestock, including cattle, zebu cattle, goats, and others. And the omnipresent chickens.

We went up a small tributary that exists only at high water. The guide explained that these few hundred yards that took only minutes to traverse today might take an hour during low water.

This section of jungle is thick with underbrush. That is in contradistinction to most other areas, where there are tall trees and a very shady, relatively empty undergrowth.

The Amazon Basin, particularly when viewed from the air, looks quite homogeneous. Actually, it is one of the most heterogeneous areas on earth! Not only are each specific region's flora and fauna extremely varied, but individual sections of the Amazon basin have differences in soil, water, climate, geology, and ecosystem.

There is an amazing variety of trees in this area: here, an occasional palm tree, there a splash of others. Trees that project above the canopy are called emergents. An interesting fact (which you'll want to observe) is that the crown of each giant tree stands alone in its own personal space; there is a gap of several feet between its crown and the next tree's. The reason for this "crown shyness" is not known.

The trees, compared to many others throughout the world, do not live very long. Even the largest exists for only about 100 years. How the trees survive long periods of time under water remains one of the many mysteries of the Amazon. Roots require oxygen for respiration. Water deeper than six to ten feet contains very little oxygen. Yet flood waters in the Amazon may rise as much as 40 feet. Only a few species grow aerial roots above the floodline. How do the trees get the oxygen they require?

The late Alwyn Gentry, botanist with the Missouri Botanical Gardens and avid researcher of the Amazon Basin, found 300 species of trees with a trunk diameter of 4 inches (10 cm) or more. This, in an area of one hectare (2 1/2 acres), near Explorama Lodge. An equivalent area in a temperate forest usually contains no more than a dozen different tree species.

Cecropia is the favorite tree of the sloth and other mammals. It is a very common tree in the Peruvian Amazon and, when flowering, also attracts many birds. The cecropia has a gray, thin trunk with leaves growing mostly near the top. The large leaves resemble a parasol. Cecropias are fast-growing trees, frequently springing up in a space where a fallen tree has left a "light gap." Often found along the river banks, they seek the sun.

In the late afternoon after a rain, we saw cecropia trees highlighted against the dark rain clouds receding toward the east. Against this backdrop, the cecropia bark glows almost luminescently in the setting sun.

The cecropia, never more than about 60 feet tall, could be called the fast food restaurants of the forest because they feed so many different birds and animals. One scientist in Mexico counted 48 different species of animals and birds that feed on these trees. Mammals eat the fruit, sloths eat the leaves, ants eat the nectar, and birds enjoy the flowers. Cecropias come in two varieties: male trees and female trees!

You will see many cecropias on your voyage, particularly on the tributaries like the Ucayali and the Tapiche. Examine each one as you pass and eventually you'll see a sloth.

Perhaps the most majestic tree in the rain forest is the kapok (*ceiba*). Growing from buttressed roots to a height of about 165 feet (50 m), it has a smooth gray trunk and a crown of branches at the top. It supports many epiphytes and lianas. The tree may grow as much as 10 feet (3 m) annually.

A kapok tree may flower only every four or five years, but when it does it produces between 500 and 4000 fruits. Each fruit contains about 200 seeds; so a single tree may yield 800,000 seeds in its production year.

The silky fibers of the kapok are used as "down" filler in items such as mattresses and life preservers.

Rubber trees, once an economic staple of the area, are still "milked" to a limited extent. Your guide will show you a rubber tree and will describe the preparation process. It is virtually the same used during the boom years from 1880 to 1912.

We returned to La Turmalina, ate another delicious lunch, and caught our daily nap.

Then, the boat landed at an interesting little village called Galicia. We walked the plank: A gangplank was extended from ship to shore so we could disembark and investigate the village. The inhabitants are ribereños, not Indians. The dozen or so families live in thatched-roofed houses on stilts. Galicia has a school, a clinic, and, to communicate with the rest of the world, a short-wave radio transmitter. The guides showed us the various fruits the natives eat; the many varieties of trees scattered throughout the village constitute their handy, front-yard orchard. The villagers demonstrated for us the method of processing manioc, the wild root which is their dietary staple.

Corn is the fastest growing of Amazonian crops: in the humid tropics it is ready for harvest in as little as two months. *Manioc* takes longer, usually six to eight months to edible size; but if unharvested, the tubers will continue to grow for up to eighteen months. Convenient underground storage, fresh when you need it. Mothers in the rain forest give a whole different meaning to "I'll dig up something for dinner."

Lively, laughing, healthy-looking children greeted us and romped about. They (and some of the adults) offered to sell us pottery, necklaces, and other items they had crafted. Theirs, however, was not the annoying, obtrusive type of marketing commonly pitched in so much of the third world .

The children were out of school this day because their school vacation is January, February, and March. Teachers are hired by the government, which assigns them to their schools for three years at a time.

Two villagers showed us their housepets: an ocelot and a dusky titi monkey. An ocelot is a small, wild cat, similar to the bobcat. Although they have been sighted in the wild on International Expedition trips, you are more likely to observe them as family pets.

CHAPTER 4

BEAUTY AND MORE BEAUTY

W̲e went for a short small-boat ride before breakfast. It was cool and foggy at first and we were serenaded with birdsongs. We saw perhaps a dozen different species of birds and some saddle-backed tamarin monkeys.

One of the smaller varieties of monkey, the saddle-backed tamarin's body is only about nine inches (22 cm) long, with a tail somewhat longer than that. Their coat consists of three distinctive markings: their black or brown upper body; the black-and-yellow striped "saddle"; and dark-brown or red hind legs. Though they live in groups of two to twelve individuals, they are difficult to spot, but they reveal their presence by their soft trilling sound or, at a distance, loud whistles. The saddle-backed tamarin stays mostly in the middle or lower levels of the forest below the canopy, although they sometimes forage for insects in knotholes and crevices of tree trunks near the ground. They also occasionally suck sap from holes made by other

monkeys. Records of the 1996 International Expedition trips show that saddle-backed tamarins were sighted on 48 percent of the trips. The percentage increased in 1997.

The trees we saw on this trip were fantastic to behold. Twisting and thrusting into a wide variety of shapes. This is the wildest area we've seen yet. The area where La Turmalina was tied up was marked as a national park.

After breakfast, we took the small boats up the Yanayacu River to a landing where International Expeditions has built a "ranger house."

Until last night, this house was occupied by a team of scientists studying the monkeys in the area. The boat returning these scientists to Iquitos passed La Turmalina in the night.

ACEER and Roberto Rotundo (the owner of La Turmalina) underwrote this comprehensive field study. This is one of the world's best observation grounds for primatologists. In addition to documenting fifteen species of primates, the scientists also found over 290 species of birds in the Rio Tapiche watershed. A major discovery was a large palm swamp that seems to be the breeding grounds for birds and mammals. It is a unique feature of the Tapiche not previously discovered and accounts for the diversity of animals seen by visitors on the river boats.

From the ranger house, we went on our first "jungle walk"—a two-and-a-half hour trek into the forest. We saw many birds, including a seldom-seen Pavonine quetzal. Alfredo was very excited at this unusual sighting. Our guide's emotional reaction to important sightings is both amusing and laudatory. It was inspiring to see a

Peruvian who fully appreciates the uniqueness of the wildlife in his homeland.

We saw monkeys, ant and termite nests, and huge beehives. These nests and hives are visible throughout the jungle, even from the boat. The guide identified them as we came upon them.

Three kinds of anteaters live in this jungle. The giant anteater and the silky anteater are seldom seen, but you may see a tamandua, or "lesser anteater." This is a two-foot (60 cm)-long anteater with a tail almost as long as its body. The tamandua's most distinguishing feature is its long, narrow head. Tamanduas are active day and night. As they feed on termites, bees, and ants, the tamandua tear apart the nests of their prey. The anteater changes its diet from ants in the high water period to termites in low water. The juicier termites supply the anteater with needed moisture.

The sound of tearing wood at night almost always leads one to a tamandua. The same sound in the daytime comes from a tamandua or a brown capuchin monkey.

Coatis (also known as coatimundis) are raccoon-like tree-dwelling creatures. They have long snouts and live in packs.

Capybara is the largest rodent in the world, weighing up to 110 pounds (50 kg). One of the Amazon's most aquatic mammals, it is the only rodent that feeds on the aquatic plants that are so abundant on the river. People living along the river eat its flesh and also keep it as a pet. It is sometimes seen on the river voyage. According to the scientist, Edward O. Wilson, it would be relatively easy to establish capybara ranches in open habitats near water.

Along this section you may see several other types of mammals: squirrels, opossums, porcupines, armadillos, rats, and other rodents including paca and agouti.

Other mammals that inhabit the jungle are wild dogs, raccoons, weasels, otters, deer, and peccaries (wild pigs).

Amazonia is inhabited by several other kinds of beasts which you probably won't see. Best known of these is the jaguar. The jaguar, a spotted member of the cat family, is closely related to the cougar or mountain lion. Though a small jaguar population still remains in the Amazon Basin, they are very rarely seen by man —"Although," a guide told me, "they see you." The jaguar is the only member of the genus *Panthera* (big cats) in the Americas, where it is considered the New World equivalent of the leopard. The jaguar's coat is basically yellowish-brown but can vary from almost-white to black. Black rosettes mark its back, and its lower tail is ringed with black. Males weigh upwards of 200 pounds (90 kg); females, 165 pounds (75 kg).

Jaguars require a habitat of dense cover (forest, brush, grass), water, and sufficient prey. In general, they range over a wide variety of tropical habitats, from montane forest and wet savannah to tropical rain forest and deciduous tropical forest. They are especially common near rivers, streams, and lagoons, and sometimes use roads and trails for travel and hunting.

Although known to feed on large prey such as deer, capybara, tapir, and peccary, jaguars are opportunistic feeders. Scientists have documented cases of jaguars feeding on sloths, armadillos, and fish.

Data suggest that these great cats are predominantly solitary. Unlike many solitary cats, however, individual jaguar's home ranges may occasionally overlap.

Your guide will point out several of the many varieties of bats inhabiting the Basin. Some of the more interesting types are fruit bats, fishing bats, and vampire bats.

The fishing bat, whose appearance makes him also known as the greater bulldog bat, is larger than most of its winged kin. By the same sonar system they use to catch insects, the bats locate fish which disturb the surface of the water. Then the bat skims the surface and gaffs the fish with its large claws.

Fruit bats pick a fruit from a tree and fly to a roost, which is frequently under a large palm leaf. The bat proceeds to chew up the fruit, spitting out the indigestible seeds and fibers. A bat uses the same roost many times, leaving piles of seeds, fibers, and feces. In fact, fruit bats are the main seed dispersers for many of the forest's plants.

Vampire bats do not suck blood, but rather nick their victims and lap up the blood. An anticoagulant in the bat's saliva prevents the blood from clotting while the animal feeds.

The smaller varieties of bats eat birds (including chickens); larger ones prey on mammals, particularly cattle which are increasingly being raised on small farms in the Amazon area. Although they have been known to nick humans on rare occasions, this need not be a concern for visitors. Be assured that on the river voyage you'll sleep in a closed, air-conditioned cabin, and on the land expedition you'll be under a mosquito net and in a wooden cabin.

Scientists have discovered that vampire bats sometimes regurgitate their "take"(the blood of their victims) to "less fortunate" brethren who have not found food. This is a particular point of interest because the sharing of food is uncommon among mammals.

Many of our travel compadres declared the sights we saw on today's walk the most beautiful we have seen. The beauty was all around us, in the flowers, trees, birds, everywhere. On some of our walks we've gone through some rather dreary stretches, but not today. One of the highlights of this most interesting trek was a demonstration of how jungle people make thatch for a roof.

Predation is a greater part of the circle of life in the Amazon than in other areas of the world. Here, an estimated 80 to 90 percent of animals are eaten by predators. Elsewhere in the world a much greater share of nature's mortality is attributable to factors such as extreme temperatures and lack of space.

Speaking of predators, the harpy eagle is among the largest of the world's eagles. It's length is 32 to 39 inches (81 to 100 cm). It has a white breast, huge, strong legs, and long-clawed talons. It is seldom seen as it is quite rare. Unlike other birds of prey, the harpy doesn't soar over the forest; instead, it makes short-burst flights from tree to tree. Then it sits on a branch. This makes the bird almost impossible to see from the ground, even when it is right overhead. The harpy eagle preys upon sloths, monkeys, and macaws.

The pygmy marmoset is the world's smallest monkey. You can cup an adult in your hand. Body length is about 6 inches (15 cm) and the tail about 8 inches (20 cm). These tiny, pale-gray creatures do not have opposable thumbs but can grasp with their long fingers. They make chirping sounds and birdlike trills.

These monkeys live low in the trees, in groups of two to six. They feed on berries, buds, fruits, and arthropods, and gnaw holes in certain trees and drink the sap that oozes out. You may be able to spot the puncture marks in the trees. You are most likely to see them if you wait near those punctures, though you can see them occasionally as you travel the river. You may also see these colorful and playful creatures in native villages, where some families keep them as pets.

Upon returning to the ranger house we were served a picnic lunch, brought to us from La Turmalina's excellent galley. And the crew also brought portable toilets for the guests—an example of how far International Expeditions goes to preserve the integrity of the rain forest.

The walk was hot and humid and we had our share of mosquitos, which are enormously successful inhabitants of the Amazon Basin. Fortunately, they are neither as aggressive nor as huge as those in many places in North America. (Alaska and New Jersey come to mind.) Amazon mosquitoes (there are some twenty varieties) are easily coped with by a good insect repellent, long-sleeved shirts, and mosquito nets if sleeping in an open cabin.

On *La Turmalina* you will travel on both whitewater and blackwater. The rivers described as whitewater are rich with silt that is washed into the water. The whitewater rivers are actually a sort of *café au lait* color.

The "black" of blackwater rivers, on the other hand, are the stains of rotting vegetation. Contrary to what the names imply, blackwater rivers are very pure, while whitewater rivers are muddy and decidedly unpotable.

The term "rain forest" was first used in 1898 by Schimper, a German botanist. The Amazonian rain forest is of the type known as lowland.

Scientists named the lowland rain forest flooded by blackwater rivers *igapó*; that flooded by whitewater is called *várzea*. This book describes a voyage mainly through *igapó*—the blackwater forest. The confluence of blackwater and whitewater rivers results in a dramatic blending of the black and the brown.

Another term you may hear is *terra firma*: the parts of the forest that are never flooded. Terra firma may not be very firm at all. It is from this type of ground that the blackwater rivers flow. Although you may hear the term used by guides and other locals, there really is very little terra firma in the Peruvian Amazon, for there are few places that do not flood: the Peruvian Amazon is a "flooded forest." River levels rise and fall dramatically, flooding extensive areas.

"Tropical rain forests are famously tangled, wet, and filled with more species of plant and animals than any other habitat on earth."

David Attenborough

When we got back to **La Turmalina** we were given the opportunity to try out paddling a dugout canoe and swimming in the black Tapiche, the Amazon tributary where we were moored.

Dugout canoes are seen frequently on the rivers. Usually hewn out of cedar, most are about 18 inches across at their widest beam. It is amazing to see entire families board them without so much *as a wobble. Yet they never seem to capsize or sink. Non-natives generally have a great deal of difficulty getting into them without spilling. Sometimes the canoes are so heavily loaded that their freeboard is only a few inches.*

After dinner our group launched out for a night trip in the open boats. The skipper turned the motor off, and in the dark, I felt as if I were spying on the jungle. Well, of course that was exactly what we were doing in the daytime—that's what we came here to do!— but somehow it felt more mysterious after dark. The stars were magnificent, the moment almost unbelievably awesome.

Do not miss an excursion into the sounds of the jungle at night! Whirs, clicks, hoots, screams, grunts—these sounds are experienced, not merely heard.

We saw a couple of juvenile spectacled caiman. These were only about three feet (1 m) long, though they are known to get up to about seven feet (2 m). Evidently the large ones are farther in the flooded forest at this time of year. Black caiman often can be seen from the boat. We also saw some frogs and a large tarantula on a tree trunk. The latter was about 5 or 6 inches (12.5 to 15 cm) across. Despite their fearsome looks and despite the stories about them, these creatures are harmless.

Night monkeys will probably not be seen on moonlit boat rides—but they certainly can be heard. They communicate in two-to four-syllable, low-pitched, owl-like hoots. Their alarm calls are soft metallic clicks, sometimes accompanied by low-pitched, resonating, tonal grunts.

As Edward O. Wilson says:

> The forest at night is an experience in sensory deprivation most of the time, black and silent as the midnight zone of a cave. Life is out there in expected abundance. The jungle teems, but in a manner mostly beyond the reach of the human senses. Ninety-nine percent of the animals find their way by chemical trails laid over the surface, puffs of odor released into the air or water, and scents diffused out of little hidden glands and into the air downwind. Animals are masters of this chemical channel, where we are idiots. But we are geniuses of the audiovisual channel, equaled in this modality only by a few odd groups (whales, monkeys, birds). So we wait for the dawn, while they wait for the fall of darkness; and because sight and sound are the evolutionary prerequisites of intelligence, we alone have come to reflect on such matters as Amazon nights and sensory modalities.

One cannot help wondering what caused the tropical rain forest to develop such an amazing diversity of plant and animal life. One theory is that the lack of stress-inducing drought and frost has allowed everything to grow. In other ecosystems, dryness and coldness are major selectors of which forms of life can survive and which cannot.

Another theory is that a long, long time ago (perhaps 100 million years in the past) South America was not linked to North America but was joined with present-day Africa, Antarctica, and Australia, forming the supercontinent known as Gondwanaland.

After this huge continent broke apart, South America existed as an island. Many life forms became extinct elsewhere but not on this isolated island continent.

Millions of years later, in the Pliocene period, the Isthmus of Panama was formed, enabling species of plants and animals to migrate to the continent to the north. Nevertheless, scientists believe that only a few species became extinct.

Further, scattered, isolated pockets served as refuges and preserves, some of which still exist today. This may have contributed to the preservation of existing species, and even to the formation of new ones.

CHAPTER 5

PIRANHA!

T his morning it rained. It was the first rain of the trip. Our first four days were completely rain-free.

As a result of stress from water-logged root systems, flooded forests characteristically contain fewer trees than well-drained ones. Trees subjected to annual flooding also tend to be somewhat shorter. When flying over the forest canopy and viewing it from above, knowledgeable persons can identify flood-prone areas. Where trees undergo substantial flooding, their green is less vivid.

Riverbank biomes differ from the interior, too, because of the banks' greater exposure to sunlight. The banks are often covered with walls of climbing vines.

Shortly before 6 a.m., we were supposed to hear a bell summoning us to an early-morning open-boat ride. We didn't hear the bell, but we did hear voices saying the boat wasn't going out because of the rain. Mary and I, being sensible people, resumed sleeping.

After we arose we learned that one boat had gone out anyway. So first we had a leisurely breakfast, then the four of us who missed the early boat went out with Alfredo, the guide.

*What a hilarious experience! This was to be a fishing outing and, by golly, Alfredo was determined to get to this! ... certain! ... spot! His obsession was like any fisherman anywhere: He just **knew** where there were lots of fish ... and **nothing** was going to prevent his getting there.*

Alfredo navigated the pilot into a small cove off the Tapiche. He desperately wanted to progress to an even smaller cove ... but the way was blocked by several logs in the water plus a veritable fence of undergrowth and small trees.

Out came the machete, and there stood Alfredo on the prow of the boat—flailing away at the rain forest. Swashing and swathing like a pirate, he swashbuckled into the mass of trees and vines. He and the boatsman tied a rope around the logs that blocked the inner cove. Towing the logs one by one, our scow backed up, deposited the logs into the river and released them to float down stream ... to the Atlantic Ocean?

After beating the bushes and towing the logs for what seemed like hours, the boatsman finally backed up. He revved the engine and prepared to force our boat into the secluded cove.

We made it!

We four passengers tried to contain ourselves over Alfredo's attack on the rain forest.

Then, it was time to fish. Although poisonous plants are used extensively in the Amazon as baits for fishing, we used as bait very small cubes of beef. We baited our hooks, which were simply granny-knotted on a line tied to a stick. This is how we fished when we were Tom Sawyer-sized boys! And that was perfectly adequate for here.

As soon as the first bait touched the water it was grabbed. By a piranha. Alfredo lifted the famously ferocious fish into the boat and carefully removed the hook. This one was only about 7 inches (17 cm) long, but we treated it with respect. We subsequently caught half a dozen piranhas and a couple of small catfish.

The piranha has powerful jaws and razor-sharp triangular teeth and is capable of killing cattle. The largest piranha is about 2 feet (60 cm) long but most are considerably smaller. There are many types. In some areas of the Amazon, these well-known meat-eating fish never bite people. Elsewhere, they may. Despite what you've heard (or seen in the movies) be assured that there is no verified report of any human ever being killed by piranhas.

Piranhas are scavengers of the river as vultures are scavengers of the land. They help keep the river clean. Wounded, sick, or weak animals and fish may be attacked and devoured by swarms of piranhas.

Tasty fish, they are; when you are in piranha territory, you will probably be served piranha. Watch out for the bones.

While we fished, we saw our first blue morpho butterfly. Later, we spotted many more. The blue morpho is one of the most dramatic sights in the Amazon rain forest. A large butterfly with a wingspread up to 5 1/2 inches (13 cm), the blue morpho is of course most notable for the brilliant blue of its wings in flight. When at rest, the blue does not show. The female displays a black border around the flashy metallic color. Blue morphos are attracted to anything bright blue, such as a cloth waved about. Take something bright blue on your journey and see if you can attract them.

Butterflies are indispensable to the Amazon's ecosystem because they pollinate many of its plants. Unlike most forest residents, they inhabit both the canopy and the lower levels. One scientist estimates that if a square kilometer of Amazonian rain forest contains about 500 species of plants, they will be fed on by about 2000 moth and butterfly caterpillars. Most types of caterpillars feed on only one or two species of host plants.

Many other butterflies, some of them quite beautiful, can be found in the Peruvian Amazon. Butterflies are very difficult to photograph, but if you should get a good photo of one that your guide can not identify, send a copy of the photo to Dr. Richard Ryel, President of International Expeditions. Dr. Ryel happens to be an avid lepidopterist and is particularly interested in the Amazon, so he'll be very interested in helping you identify your find. Perhaps you'll discover a new species!

On this most interesting fishing trip we saw on a tree trunk a wooly substance which Alfredo identified as a caterpillar. It must have been as long as the fish we caught!

On our return to La Turmalina, we headed into a side channel and spotted a hoatzin. A few yards away was a nest with one of the strange birds sitting on it. Apparently, there were eggs in the nest.

The hoatzin is a crested pheasant-like bird with olive-colored plumage. It is about the size of a chicken. It has a blue face, with a fan-shaped, spiked crest. It looks like an entrant in a punk hairdo contest.

The rare hoatzin (ho-AHT-zin) is of great interest to scientists. It is the only existing bird that appears to retain vestiges of the *Archaeopteryx*, the Jurassic period's most famous fossil. Actually, the hoatzin is not related to the ancient creature at all, but probably descended from a cuckoo-like ancestor.

The young hoatzins rest in trees overhanging the various rivers of the basin. From there they drop into the waters to retrieve the fruits that fall into the river—or to escape predators. Then they climb back into the trees, using the claws on their wings like a lineman's boot hooks. These claws disappear as the young mature.

International Expeditions by Mason Fischer

Hoatzins are primitive-looking birds who build communities of large, untidy nests in branches overhanging water. Loud, gregarious and ungainly birds, hoatzins, with virtually no predators and a diet of vegetation, have little need of flying skills. Which is a good thing, because they are very awkward fliers.

Hoatzins are highly adapted to feed on leaves. They have a double crop (a sac-like enlargement in or near the gullet) where food is stored prior to digestion. It is the equivalent to the second stomach in cattle. This crop, when full, comprises over ten percent of the hoatzin's weight. The leaves in its crop ferment and give off a fetid smell that leads to the bird's nickname, stink-bird.

The fascinating hoatzin is seen on 85 to 90 percent of the trips, both the river voyage and the land expedition.

Upon leaving the inlet with the hoatzin, we stopped to admire some oropendola nests. They are fashioned in a sort of hanging basket that is quite distinct from most bird nests. They hang from the tips of tree branches, with several dozen to a tree.

These birds, a relative of orioles and about the size of a robin, provide an excellent example of the interspecies synergy that so characterizes the Amazon. Oropendola chicks are often infested by the eggs of an insect called the botfly. Since the birds themselves have no defense against the nasty botfly, they build their nests under a colony of even nastier bees, called trigonid bees. The bees keep the botflies away, and they also harass other birds, including large toucans. In similar fashion, many species of plants and animals have evolved to cooperate and thus survive.

On the afternoon trip today we saw sloths, hanging in trees and silhouetted against the sky. I find the sloth a fascinating creature. Resembling monkeys, their movements are more like that of a statue than of the active, tree-hopping primates.

Sloths live in trees; it is said that sometimes a sloth will spend its entire life in a single tree. A herbivore, it survives on leaves, particularly of the cecropia tree. There is a three-toed species and a two-toed variety. It is not widely hunted, since some Indian cultures hold it sacred. Due to its fairly open habitat and slow-to-nil speed of movement, it is much easier to spot and photograph than birds or monkeys. You'll almost certainly see sloths on the river voyage, and possibly on the land expedition as well. One was spotted swimming in the Amazon on our river voyage. This is not common.

Their now-extinct relatives, the huge prehistoric ground sloths, once ranged into what is now North America. The modern model has a rounded head, inconspicuous ears, and a flattened face. They measure up to 27 inches (70 cm) long. The forelimbs, which are longer than the hind limbs, have long, curved claws. According to the locals, sloths clasp branches so tightly that when they die their bodies continue hanging there until they decompose. They are seldom seen on the ground, since they can't walk. They can only drag themselves around with their claws.

The sloths' leisurely existence fits their biology. It was designed to be ... well, slothful. Their metabolism runs at about half the rate of most mammals'. Their body temperature is lower, too, and rather than use energy to keep themselves warm, they climb to the top of a tree and let the sun heat them up. This thermoregulation is not unlike that of many reptiles. Their digestive processes are so slow that food may remain in their body for as long as a month. If a sloth is unable to locate tender leaves and a place in the sun, its digestion could slow down so much that it would starve on a full stomach. A sloth requires one hundred hours to digest a stomachful of leaves. Because of its extremely slow metabolism, the sloth defecates only every week or so. Sloths are very difficult to keep in zoos, so those you see on your Amazon trip may be the only ones you ever see.

The three-toed sloth and the cecropia tree it lives on give another example of the synergistic relationships along the Amazon River. A sloth's coat harbors hundreds of moths and a blue-green algae that lives in its fur. The resultant coloration may protect it from its major predator, the harpy eagle. A sloth, which is about the size of a large house cat, may weigh only 10 pounds (4+ kg), but be home to a thousand moths. These moths, in turn, have their life cycle completely tied to the sloth's.

Apparently for the convenience of the moths, the sloth climbs slowly down the tree, digs a small depression with its tail at the foot of the tree, and defecates into it. This not only supplies a modicum of nutrient for the cecropia tree, but provides a place for the moths and other insects to lay their eggs. The moths fly off the sloth, lay their eggs in the dung and fly back onto the slow-moving animal as it begins its climb back up the tree. The eggs hatch, and the young insects find their way to another sloth to live on.

There are different varieties of birds to be seen on every open-boat trip, plus those that can be spotted from *La Turmalina* itself. One usually doesn't see a large quantity of any one bird, but rather only one or two of each species.

There are simply too many species of birds in the Peruvian Amazon to cover them all in this book, though we describe a few of the more spectacular ones. [Note to potential authors: A bird book is needed.] On our riverboat voyage our group recorded 99 different species in our eight-day trip. The guides said some groups record as many as 300!

Several varieties of parrots will be seen on your trips. Most have large heads, short necks, and strong feet with two front and two back toes (for climbing and grasping). They are primarily green in color. Related species include the parakeets and macaws.

Macaws are colorful and noisy birds usually seen in small flocks. Toucans, whose huge bills make them look so bizarre, vary in size from the jay-sized toucanets to the 24 inch (60 cm) white-throated toucans of the Amazon Basin. Their enormous, often brilliantly colored, canoe-shaped bills are adapted to cutting up fruits and berries. You are certain to see toucans at any time of the year. The bill on some varieties is actually longer than the bird's body.

Back to this afternoon's trip. First, a walk through an almost flooded jungle, then a boat ride up the Sabena Creek. The channel was extremely narrow with overhanging trees and vines that made a beautiful picture.

There are three types of jungle vines.

First, the lianas are rope-like hangings from tree crowns. It must have been lianas that Tarzan swung on through the forest. Actually, you probably could not swing on most of them unless you were as light as a monkey, though they may hold your weight for a short time. Some lianas, though, are as thick and strong as a six or eight inch (15 to 20 cm) tree trunk. Old, large lianas indicate an undisturbed primary forest.

Lianas actually begin life as a shrub. They grow toward a tree, then up its trunk until they dangle from the crown. Though the tree supports the weight of the mature plant, liana roots remain in the ground. As your guide will show you, lianas contain drinkable water.

A second type of vine is the climber. Like the lianas, they germinate in the ground and then grow toward a tree. Unlike lianas, though, climbers' roots become anchored to the tree.

Perhaps the best-known vine is the much-maligned strangler fig. It germinates from a seed a bird or monkey drops on a tree. At this stage it is an epiphyte—it derives nutrients and moisture from the air, without benefit of roots. The vine grows down the tree trunk, toward the ground. When it reaches the ground it establishes its own root system. As it grows it wraps itself around the trunk, fusing into a sort of mesh. It not only constricts the tree it grows around, it makes such a heavy shade the tree cannot photosynthesize. So the tree dies and decomposes, a victim of strangulation and lack of light. This leaves the strangler fig standing alone. You will see many examples of this in the forest.

Many so-called vines are actually aerial roots of epiphytes, especially philodendrons.

Although it rained in the morning and was still threatening when we started out after lunch, the skies cleared by the end of the afternoon trip. Amazon rains seldom last for more than an hour or two.

This evening we took another night trip, but this one was not as exciting as last night's. We did see five Muscovy ducks swimming on the river. Many of the ribereños raise ducks, but we saw few wild ones.

Mary Lutz

Mary Lutz

CHAPTER 6

DOLPHINS FOR BREAKFAST

A rising early, we took off around 6 a.m. to have breakfast in the middle of Iberia Lake. It is one of the many ox-bow lakes scattered throughout the river system.

As we ate sandwiches, rolls, fruit, coffee, and tea, an entertaining troupe of leaping dolphins gave a surround-around performance. Fresh-water dolphins like the ox-bow lakes because the fish that are their chief food source are frequently found there.

While we were anchored and eating, we were approached by two dugout canoes with a couple of fishermen in each. One of the entrepreneurs sold our guide a fish—which we later had for dinner. In the manner of fishermen everywhere showing off their huge catch, they displayed the five-foot (150 cm) paiche they caught. The paiche (or arapaima) ranks among the top two or three largest freshwater fishes in the world. It weighs up to 325 lbs (146 kg) and may exceed 9 feet (3 m) in length. Due to overfishing, these huge specimens are rare now and our guides' admiration indicated that our fishermen friends' catch was quite braggable.

Today, the paiche is an important food source for the people living in Amazonia, but the early Indians did not utilize it extensively. It is caught mainly by harpoons or gillnets, and was difficult for the pre-fishing gear fishermen to catch. Another problem—without refrigeration or salt how does one preserve such a huge fish? The paiche is one of several fish in the Amazon that breathes air in addition to breathing under water. This peculiar trait has apparently evolved so it can prey in the deoxygenated water of the low-water period of the river.

After having breakfast we took off around the lake and witnessed a gulp (flock) of cormorants. There were at least hundreds, maybe thousands. Cormorants are diving birds. When a large flock of cormorants roosts in trees, their feces can actually kill vegetation.

This morning we saw five different types of monkeys.

Red howler monkeys travel in troops whose chorus is said to be one of the strangest sounds in nature. A male calls with a series of deep grunts which accelerate, then expand into a prolonged roar. Then the females join with their higher-pitched calls. The howls are produced by forcing air through a cavity in a bone at the base of their tongue. This howling, which goes for many minutes, is usually heard at dawn, late afternoons, or during rainstorms.

This is one of the larger monkeys you'll see here. The adult male is about 24 inches (60 cm) in body length, its prehensile tail approximately the same. Much of its body is red, in shades varying from red-orange to dark red, while its back coloration comes from the bright orange-to-gold palette.

Red howlers have a small brain and a scarcely developed social order. Mostly, they stay in the upper canopy, and couch potato-like, they don't move around much. Except for their howling, they are relatively inconspicuous, but you can tell where they've been by their plentiful droppings which have a strong, stablelike smell. When alarmed, they defecate and urinate on whatever/whoever's below.

Tour logs note that howlers were seen on 77 percent of the voyages in 1996 and on almost all trips in 1997.

International Expeditions by Mason Fischer

Brown capuchin monkeys have dark caps, limbs, and tail, and a dark bar in front of their ears. Adults are a foot to a foot and a half in length (30 to 45 cm), their prehensile tail about the same. The noisy brown capuchins may be the most common monkeys in Amazonia. They emit frequent short yipping whines, but their alarm call is two-toned, rather like a bird whistle. They forage for vegetation, which they noisily tear apart, and for small animals. Active in the daytime, they travel in groups of 5 to 20. In 1996, they were seen on 65 percent of the riverboat trips.

White-fronted capuchin monkeys are similar to brown capuchins in size and habits, but they are lighter hued and a little less noisy and destructive, which makes them harder to sight. Their pink face is fringed with silvery-white. The white-fronted capuchin is a slender fellow, while the brown variety is stocky and robust. The white-fronted are less destructive than browns, but more difficult to approach.

Capuchins are very intelligent animals and appear to be observing, even jeering, the humans watching them. Which doesn't happen often, as capuchins are seldom seen by travelers.

The dusky titi monkey is a small fellow, only about a foot (30 cm) in length, with long, soft, glossy fur which comes in shades of dark brown, gray, reddish, or black. Its flat face is set in a small, round head. It uses its long, furry tail for balance while moving. A daytime creature, the dusky titi eats leaves, fruit, bird eggs, and insects. It prefers swampy terrain. There is a good chance you will see a dusky titi on either trip.

The brown, muscular woolly monkeys have a body length of about a foot and a half (45 cm), and a two-foot-long (60 cm) tail. The fur is dense and short, giving them the woolly look that gives them their name. They are active during the day and travel in groups up to about 60. Males may threaten humans by shaking branches and defecating. They will be found in the upper and middle levels of the trees. They are rarely seen.

The red uakari monkey has a body length of two feet (60 cm), but a tail length of only six inches (15 cm)—the only New World monkey with a short tail. Its most distinguishing features are its bright orange upper parts and bright red face, and its "ca-ca-ca-ca." Red uakaris travel in large groups in the middle and upper parts of the forests, except in low water when they may be found on the ground. In either case, they are seldom seen.

Primatologists can identify species or subspecies from just the animal's fur. This type of analysis can be done in the wild.

Besides seeing the monkeys and some sloths we observed some hawks mating, another bird building a nest, and a rare bird called an orange-backed troupial.

The ability of the guides to spot birds or mammals was a continuing source of wonder to all our group. It was a humbling experience to witness these men in action. They seemed to be able to sense the presence of living things worth seeing without even seeing them! One of the guides, Rene, grew up in a small village along a tributary of the Amazon. He learned to stalk and hunt birds and small animals at a very young age. Besides having spent years engaged in this type of spotting, the guides know in what areas or even in what trees particular species are likely to be seen. An individual visiting the Amazon without a guide would miss a great deal.

Another guide, Ari, is an Indian. Rene, Ari, and our third guide, Alfredo, speak excellent English. Ari is also good at fixing broken cameras.

The afternoon trip was a fairly short one to Jesus de Paz, a ribereño village. Only eight families lived there. To us, the school was the village's most interesting feature. Though school was not in session at this time, children and adults gathered there to take a gander at the visitors. We crowded into the schoolroom, which, if you rounded up the measurement you could stretch it to 20 ft x 20 ft (6 m x 6 m). The furnishings were certainly spartan: only some crude desks and a few maps on the wall indicated that it was a schoolroom. The children sang for us, and in return, we sang "America, the Beautiful" for them.

Jesus de Paz boasts a village church. Our guide explained that the religion in this village, as in most of the villages in this part of the Amazon, is a combination of Catholic and Evangelical.

One of the first Catholic priests in the area was a Jesuit from Bohemia, **Father Samuel Fritz**. He served the Indians from 1686 to 1723, converting four Indian tribes including the Omagua. At one time Father Fritz had a parish of some fifty villages scattered over a thousand-mile area. A heroic figure, he was idolized by the Indians. In addition to surviving the perils of the Amazon, his work was plagued by slave-trade raiders, some of whom were aided by Carmelite missionaries. When Father Fritz died his body was found to be scarred by insect bites, as he had never slapped a mosquito nor brushed off any other insect, accepting of any punishment God gave him.

Despite all the difficulties facing him, and despite his lack of scientific expertise or instruments, Father Fritz was the first man to draw an accurate map of the Amazon.

The Carmelites, and some of the other Catholic orders, supported (or tolerated) the institution of slavery and the slave traders' raids to capture Indians to sell. In all fairness it should be reported that the Carmelites inoculated residents of their missions. That probably saved the lives of thousands of Indians.

In 1750, an estimated 25,000 Indians lived in Jesuit missions (called Reductions) in the upper Amazon. The Franciscans operated additional missions. A number of Indian uprisings occurred in the 16th and 17th centuries. Shortly thereafter the Jesuit empire began to crumble, both in Europe and in South America. The Jesuits left South America in 1767.

Many of those missions still exist, but now several other religions have established themselves in the area, so that the mix of religions is little different in the Peruvian Amazon than in the rest of Peru.

There is still a controversy about the role of the Jesuits in the development of the Amazon. On one hand, they fought against slavery and upheld the humanness of the indigenous people. On the other hand, they tried to destroy the Indian cultures and imposed a rigid discipline on the native people.

In 1913 the Catholic Church expanded its role in the upper Amazon when Franciscan monks established missions in the former rubber-producing areas. They left in 1917, saying they could do no more good for the Indians. At this stage in history, Protestant missionaries were not allowed in Peru.

However, in the 1940s the Wycliffe Bible Translators, a Protestant group, established

"Theirs (the Jesuits) was an astounding achievement; to civilize, convert and administer most of an unexplored continent with only a handful of men armed with nothing but faith, must be a feat without parallel in human history."

Robin Furneaux

their home base near Pucallpa on the Ucayali River. From there they spread their missions into many areas of the Peruvian Amazon.

Leaving the village, we returned to La Turmalina for another excellent dinner. On the way back, our guide spotted a small bird in the distance that he identified as a Paradise jacamar. He said it is relatively rare in this region as it is a native of Brazil, which he estimated is about 150 miles (240 km) east.

Alfredo Chavez told me that La Turmalina is owned by Señor Roberto Rotundo, who was once Minister of Tourism for Peru. The guide referred to him as "Mr. Peru." Rotundo is reportedly a very remarkable individual—he only sleeps three hours a night—and quite an entrepreuner. He also owns La Esmeralda, another boat used by International Expeditions on its tours out of Iquitos.

CHAPTER 7

IQUITOS

*T*his is the day we returned to Iquitos
We spent the early morning getting
ready to disembark. In other words,
packing, taking pictures, saying goodbye, etc.

La Turmalina *traveled all night, this time
with the current assisting rather than hindering.
On our upstream journey, the boat was anchored
at night, but now it was as if it was eager to gt
home and refused to be reined in. As they say, "a
horse speeds up as it gets near the barn."*

*We were ahead of schedule for our arrival at
Iquitos, so we docked at Tamashiyacu (pop. 4000),
near Iquitos. Here, we saw signs of civilization.
Some of the streets were paved, there were some
streetlights, and even a few TV antennas! Our
group visited the local library and a cabinetmaker's
shop.*

*Arriving in Iquitos around 3 p.m., we were
transported by air-conditioned bus to the Hotel
Victoria Regia. Although clean and with satisfac-
tory amenities, the hotel didn't seem nearly as
comfortable as* La Turmalina. *If home is where
the heart is, I guess we had come to feel* La
Turmalina *was home.*

Iquitos was founded in 1739 by a Jesuit priest. The town grew slowly: a hundred years later it had only about sixty inhabitants. About 1880, with the advent of the rubber boom, Iquitos sprang to life. Rubber barons imported statues, marble, and even a whole steel building from the Paris Exhibition. That building, designed by the architect of the Eiffel Tower, stands today in downtown Iquitos. Some of the Portuguese tiles that were imported still remain on buildings.

After the boom collapsed around 1912, Iquitos became almost a ghost town. Today, with its several hundred thousand inhabitants, it booms once again. Here is the headquarters of a large Peruvian military garrison. The city is built along the shore of the Amazon—which has eroded the banks until Iquitos is almost an island.

In many ways Iquitos is a typical Latin American city. The difference is its isolation: there are no roads linking it to the rest of the world. Everything in Iquitos was made there or brought in by boat or plane. Local streets were not paved until 1951, when the U.S. Navy sold a surplus LST (Landing Ship-Tank) to Peru. In Callao (seaport city for Lima, Peru's capital) the ship was loaded with 2800 tons (2520 metric tons) of gravel. Sailing up the west coast of South America, through the Panama Canal and up the Amazon to Iquitos, the ship sailed 7,000 miles (11,200 km) to bring paving material to a city 650 miles (1040 km) away.

Although 2300 miles (3680 km) from the ocean, Iquitos is only about 300 feet (92 m) above sea level. This altitude is one-quarter of the height of the Empire State Building. The discovery of oil west of Iquitos in 1971 resulted in the city fathers declaring a two-day holiday. One of the sad facts about Iquitos is the presence of a major oil off-loading facility and refinery. This is a notorious polluter in the immediate area.

Despite its isolation, Iquitos is a bustling metropolis with a busy airport. Its most evident feature is the prevalence of three wheeled motorcycles called 'motokars,' most of which are used as taxis. There are weekly flights to Miami (four hours) and daily flights to Lima, Peru's capitol (an hour and a half). Yet right outside the city is the jungle. Here is an international airport— with jungle adjoining the runway.

Iquitos has been free of the terrorist activities that have plagued other parts of Peru for years. This is because Peruvians must show identification papers in order to travel by plane. Since terrorists usually don't have such documents, they don't come to Iquitos.

Iquitos (perhaps all of Peru) has an interesting method of taking census. A Sunday is designated as Census Day and the entire populace is required to stay in their homes until census-takers come to count them. If a person leaves his or her home before being counted, he is subject to arrest!

In addition to the well-known rubber boom, the region has experienced several other lesser industrial booms. Exports have included animal skins, leche caspi from which chewing gum is made; vegetable ivory, used for making buttons and chess pieces before plastics came along; barbasco, used to make rotenone for insecticides; and rosewood oil. Some crude oil has been taken from Peru in recent years but certainly not to the extent of, say, Ecuador or Venezuela. Large-scale timber harvesting has never been as major an activity in the Peruvian Amazon as in Brazil.

The major reason for the lack of timber harvesting is that Iquitos is the most expensive ocean shipping port in the world. Remember, it is 2300 miles (3680 km) from the sea. This fact is responsible for the uncut quality of the Peruvian Amazon.

On the outskirts of downtown Iquitos is Belen, where thousands of people live on boats or floating shacks in extremely unhygienic conditions. They are obviously very poor. Belen really is both a slum and a market.

Walking around the city of Iquitos was particularly interesting because it was a Saturday. In the afternoon we took a brief tour of the Belen market, the largest floating market on the Amazon. Among the many strange items for sale in this chaotic and dirty marketplace were native medications and alligator tails—which are illegal to possess or sell but there is little, if any, enforcement of these laws.

Some people living in Belen, or elsewhere on the river, build their houses on stilts or on floating platforms, house-boat style, so they are seldom flooded out.

Iquitos is also a center for the exportation of wild animals, including tropical fish. Much of this trade is illegal.

Angelfish is the common name of several freshwater and saltwater fishes. They include the scalare, a popular aquarium fish native to the Amazon and Guiana. Less than 6 inches

(15 cm) long, it is silver with gray or black bars. There are also types of bright-colored tropical fish, especially the angelichthys, an edible fish weighing up to 4 pounds (almost 2 kg). Other fish shipped to tropical fish stores in the U.S. and elsewhere are silver carp, neon tetras, and piranhas.

In the evening International Expeditions hosted dinner on the town. We were honored guests at the La Olla de Oro (The Pot of Gold) Restaurant in Iquitos, owned by the parents of the young man who manages the dining room on **La Turmalina**. *The banners and balloons festooning the restaurant indicated this was a special, party-mode occasion.*

Dinner guests included most members of our tour group and our guides, plus scientists who had been studying the monkeys up the Rio Tapiche. A Peruvian band and two dancers entertained us. After our excellent meal, our servers brought out a cake with **La Turmalina** *written in icing.*

The next day we visited the arts and crafts shop operated by guide Alfredo Chavez's mother. Alfredo himself does some wood carving which is for sale in this shop. Many of the products for sale, though, are from Indian artisans. Prominent among these are the various items made by the Shipibo Indians. Famed for the geometric designs of their art work, the shy Shipibo can be found living along the Ucayali and the Tapiche.

From Iquitos the Amazon falls very gradually to the ocean, about 1 1/2 inches per mile (6 cm per kilometer). It has been likened to a bathtub draining.

The remarkable infertility of the soil is explained by three factors: geological antiquity, warm temperatures, and heavy rainfall. When the warm rainwater percolates through the ground it dissolves whatever minerals are in the soil and carries them into the river.

The diversity of Amazonian lifeforms create an interesting variety of methods of plant pollination. Bees and other insects are undoubtedly the major carriers of pollen but monkeys, birds, bats, rodents, and other vertebrates also do their part. In temperate forests, wind is the primary carrier of pollen, but it is less of a factor in tropical rain forests like the Amazon.

Certain bees travel several miles in the course of a normal day. Researchers have discovered that, although some species of bees visit many different plants in the course of a year, they usually carry pollen of only one plant at any one time.

The specialized structure of flowers and other plants is such that the plants attract the specific type of pollinator which they need. A plant's odor, color, and shape draw the pollinator which is best for their species.

For example, one vine (*Aristolochia*), has trumpet-like flowers with mottled, shiny red, fleshy lobes at the throat of the trumpet. The combination of its fleshy appearance and its foul, rotting-protein smell attracts carrion flies. The flies enter the tube of the trumpet but, trapped by the hairs inside, are unable to back out. Thus they fly around inside the central cavity, inadvertently collecting pollen. Later the hairs at the entrance wilt, freeing the flies to escape and deposit the pollen elsewhere.

"Although at first glance the jungle seems to be a totally disorganized chaos of superabundant greenery, closer examination shows that it has a definite structure. Tall trees, short trees, vines, and epiphytes each have a specific role in the general scheme of things. And animal life in turn is well fitted into the overall architecture of the rain forest. In the jungle, in short, there is a place for everything—and everything remains pretty much in its place."

Paul W. Richards

CHAPTER 8

EXPLORAMA LODGE

W e left Iquitos this morning and traveled down the Amazon to Explorama Lodge. The trip took about an hour and a half. Our boat was similar to a bus in that it had individual seats, was covered from the weather, but had no toilet facilities. Fourteen people took this trip, which was the first leg of the land expedition. Our solitary guide for this venture was named Ari.

Explorama Lodge is a primitive jungle lodge, and yet given that, it is not unattractive or uncomfortable. The buildings are of unplaned lumber, which certainly lends a rustic air. Walkways are on raised platforms to avoid the Amazon mud. The meals are good. Not up to the quality of the meals on board **La Turmalina**, perhaps, but certainly good for camp fare. Although there is no electricity or running water each room has kerosene lanterns and washbasins with bottled drinking water available. The lanterns and water supply are refilled daily. For the showers, river water is pumped into tanks. Numerous flowers and interesting plants grow about the complex. Although the windows and doors are not screened, good mosquito netting is provided over the comfortable beds.

Several tame parrots roost on the roofbeams outside the dining room, begging crackers from diners as they leave. Hammocks on the sort-of porch offer languid lounging.

There were several groups staying at the lodge, perhaps 60 people in all.

Shortly after lunch, Ari led us on a two-and-a-half-hour hike. He carefully explained many things about the forest. I can't say enough about the quality of the guides. The three native guides I traveled with spoke English well; they had learned from scientists as well as growing up in the Amazon basin, and had years of experience as guides. They all enjoyed showing, and teaching about, the fascinating forest. Alfredo, Reni, and Ari were tremendous assets to my learning and experiencing the Peruvian Amazon.

"This (the Amazon), the most diverse flora in the world, has been the least studied by aboriginal and by Caucasian biologists."

Dr. James
            Duke
(personal
communica-
            tion)

It is estimated that as many as one quarter of the plants in the upper Amazon are epiphytes—plants that grow on other plants. Epiphytes include mosses, lichens, ferns, cacti, bromeliads, orchids, and many others. It is estimated that 28,000 species of epiphytes exist throughout the world. One study counted 15,500 of them in Central and South America.

Epiphytes are not really parasites, in that their roots do not penetrate the host plant's tissues. They may, however, compete for light and nutrients and thus be destructive to the

Mary Lutz

International Expeditions by Dick Mills

International Expeditions by Mason Fischer

International Expeditions by Dick Mills

International Expeditions by Richard Ryel

International Expeditions by Mason Fischer

International Expeditions by Mason Fischer

host plant. In any one tree the total leaf area of the epiphytes may exceed the leaf area of the host tree. It is true that epiphytes exist in temperate forests as well as tropical, but there is a basic difference between the two. In the temperate zone most epiphytes are mosses or lichens that can endure temperature extremes. Rain forest epiphytes, though, not only include these life forms but also a great many flowering plants.

These "gardens in the air" play their own essential role in the order of things. They trap debris and moisture, thus providing shelter for small animals such as insects and frogs, some of which live their entire lives in these aerial gardens.

Rather surprisingly, many epiphytes have characteristics in common with desert plants. In periods of no rain, some epiphytes shut down their metabolism until the next deluge, thus conserving their moisture.

Certain orchids reduce their roots and leaves to small strands in order to cut down water loss. Since their smaller leaves trap less of the sun's energy, they, therefore, invest their leaves with chlorophyll, which gives them a green appearance and enables them to photosynthesize. Most orchids are epiphytes but some are terrestrial.

Some epiphytes have roots like sponges which they dangle beneath their branches and soak up moisture from the air. And so it goes.

Bromeliads are tree-dependent plants . Most of them reproduce from seeds. Some bromeliads are terrestrial, most notably the pineapple.

Some have an unusual method of trapping moisture in the canopy—they are little water tanks. Not surprisingly, these are known as tank bromeliads. Their leaves are closely overlapped at the base, channeling raindrops into the center. A large bromeliad can hold as much as a bucket of water. Snails, crabs, earthworms, small snakes, lizards, salamanders, and other creatures can be found in bromeliads. One study found 250 species in these plants.

The weight of all these epiphytes and the water they collect can run to several tons per tree and, as you would expect, after a rainfall tree branches sometimes plummet to the ground. Nearly half of all the nutrients in the rain forest canopy may be extracted from the air by epiphytes. These are from the nutrients in dust particles or dissolved in rain.

Scientists have studied the Amazon basin for centuries. A few are particularly noteworthy:

Baron Alexander von Humboldt (1769-1859) was a wealthy, well-connected "renaissance man" from Berlin. He was the most influential of the early botanists to explore South America. Arriving in northern South America in 1799, he and his companion Aime Bonpland spent the next five years mapping portions of the area. Baron von Humboldt gathered some 60,000 plants, along with an astonishing array of other scientific data. Included among his achievements was his climb of Chimborazo, the huge volcano in what is today Ecuador. His ascent, just a little short of the summit, was to an elevation higher than man had ever been at that time. Humboldt was the first to verify that the Orinoco and the Amazon rivers were linked, thus establishing it as earth's largest river basin. The Humboldt current, which flows off the western coast of South America, was named for the baron.

Alfred Russel Wallace (1823-1913) was an English naturalist who spent four years exploring the Amazon and its tributaries. In 1854 he published *Travels on the Amazon and Rio Negro.* Wallace later went to the Malay Archipelago for eight years; while there he developed his theory of natural selection in evolution, which Charles Darwin had come up with independently.

Henry Bates (1825-1892) and **Richard Spruce** (1817-1893) were two of the nineteenth century explorers and scientists who did much to uncover the scientific wealth of the Amazon Basin. Spruce was responsible for locating and exporting the seeds of *cascarilla roja*, the red bark tree, from which quinine is made. Quinine has saved millions of lives throughout the world by stopping the ravages of malaria. Quinine was perhaps the first of the great benefits to mankind to come out of the interior of South America. The second was rubber which will be discussed later.

Cooperation between species occurs throughout nature, not just in the rain forest. But on a far more limited scale than in the rain forest. The rain forest—and the Amazon is the largest in the world—is the pre-eminent example of interspecies cooperation. This is a chief reason scientists, particularly botanists, find the Amazon so fascinating.

Many Amazonian flowers are red. Some birds, especially hummingbirds, are attracted to red; therefore, flowers are more likely to find themselves pollinated if they produce red blossoms. Many "red" flowers are really

"To label Amazonia an ecosystem of fantastic complexity, infinite diversity, and marvelous integration is barely to do justice to this masterpiece of natural selection."

Betty J. Meggers, Anthropologist

not red at all, but have red leaves. Heliconia, for example, looks red and yellow, but the flowers are actually purple or blue.

Scientists speculate that the reason many fruits are yellow or orange in color is that their seeds are dispersed by monkeys or bats—and monkeys and bats are red-green color blind. They can differentiate between green foliage and orange or yellow flowers, but cannot discern red flowers amid the greenery.

Many rain forest plants have narrow, downward-pointing tips to their leaves. These "drip tips" hasten the loss of water from the leaves, an important feature in the ever-moist rain forest. If water were to remain on the leaves it would leach out nutrients and encourage epiphyte growth, either of which would eventually harm the plant.

One of the most-used plants in the Amazon is the achiote. This bears a small, pear-like fruit which, when opened, reveals a yellow-orange pigment. Locally, the pigment is used as a face paint. In Europe and America it is a dye to color butter and margarine.

Another interesting facet of the Amazon are the Indian legends. Here's one:

The great potoo is a nocturnal bird related to the whip-poor-will, though somewhat larger. The song of the great potoo sounds like "ay-ay-ma-ma". Understandably, the natives call this the ayaymama bird. Local lore tells a legend about this bird.

There once was a happy family consisting of a husband, wife, and two sons. The wife died of jungle fever and, after several months of grieving, the husband married again. His second wife turned out to be a classic "evil stepmother." She convinced the man to take his two sons into the jungle and abandon them there. The unfortunate boys starved to death but, at the moment of their death, were transformed into ayaymama birds. Every night from then on they returned to their village and taunted their evil stepmother with the call "ay-ay-ma-ma." This ultimately drove the woman to commit suicide. The calls of the ayaymama (or great potoo) continue to be heard in the jungle, reminding all parents of their obligation to their children.

At dinner that evening we met the vivacious doctor, Linnea Smith, and the resident artist, David. In return for their services, Explorama Lodge provides each of them housing, meals, and transportation. Fifteen minutes travel from the lodge, the doctor has a little clinic where she treats the local people and lodge employees. She also is the physician for the guests at Explorama Lodge.

The Wisconsin-born Dr. Smith has lived near Explorama Lodge for some six years, and until recently, has worked on a purely voluntary basis. Her clinic was built by the Duluth, Minnesota Rotary Club.

A book about her experiences has been written by Dr. Smith. Titled **La Doctora**, *it is published by Pfeifer-Hamilton of Duluth, Minnesota.*

David, the artist, is from Australia. He is spending three months here simply because he is enamored of the Amazon.

That night we slept so well we missed the plummeting deluge pouring from the sky.

CHAPTER 9

THE GREAT RUBBER BOOM

*B*efore breakfast we took a short boat-hop to an excellent bird-watching area. We saw many interesting birds in the field. We also saw some squirrel monkeys a distance away.

When we had been on **La Turmalina**, we didn't have to go anywhere at all to spot some squirrel monkeys: we watched them through the dining room window.

Squirrel monkeys, the most common primate in the Amazon Basin, have olive or grayish crowns and a body length of a foot or so (30 cm). The nonprehensile tail is 16 inches (40 cm). They are active during the day. These monkeys are found in large groups of twenty to 100. They troop single file after a leader along constantly used pathways in the trees. Very agile, they have been known to catch insects on the wing. They were spotted on every 1996 Ucayali-Tapiche voyage, and are frequently seen on the land expedition as well.

After breakfast we went for another hike in the rain forest. Ari warned it would be quite muddy from last night's rain. "Quite muddy" was an understatement. Part of the trail was actually under water; we had to wade in water nearly up to our knees. In addition, during the night a tree had fallen on the underwater trail. The members of the group kidded Ari for not anticipating that the trail would be flooded.

On today's morning walk we saw two horned screamers. These birds are common to this area but are found only in South America. About a yard long, these goose-like birds are seen walking on floating vegetation. Their call is more of a gargled hoot than a scream.

Ari showed us a rubber tree and described how the sap of this tree is processed into rubber.

The Great Rubber Boom took place from roughly 1880 to 1912. It resulted in a temporary boost to the economy of the area but also effected a dramatic drop in the indigenous population.

Julio César Arana (1864-1952) was the most famous rubber baron of the Great Rubber Boom. During this period, rubber was becoming an important product worldwide and most of it came from the Amazon.

Some of the entrepreneurs who owned the rubber-tree forests were ruthless individuals who hired native Indians and then treated them as virtual slaves. Many instances were recorded of torture, rape, and killings.

Arana was a Peruvian who lived in Iquitos. In 1905 he bought a huge estate in the Colombian part of the Amazon Basin. His property was along the Rio Putumayo, just east of the Rio Napo, which today forms the border between Peru and Colombia. An estimated 50,000 Indians lived in the area his estate occupied. Arana's company almost succeeded in wiping them out.

Most of the rubber gathering area along the Putumayo was in what is today Colombian territory. However, the border was claimed and occupied by both Peru and Colombia before the dispute was finally settled in 1922. Moreover, the infamous Arana had his headquarters in Iquitos, which meant the operation was in Colombia, its headquarters in Peru. It would be easy enough for each country to claim they had jurisdiction and for Arana to claim neither had.

Arana hired overseers, mostly criminals and deviants from Barbados, who were expected to see to it that a quota of rubber was collected at any cost. The Indians, virtually slaves, frequently failed to obtain these unrealistic quotas. They were then tortured. If they escaped, they were hunted down and killed, presumably as a lesson to others. The torture and killing escalated, probably because of the sadistic tendencies of the overseers.

It is not clear how much of this killing was encouraged by Arana himself, but he could not have helped but know of it.

As rubber production soared the Indian population in the Putumayo area dropped. An estimated fifty thousand dwindled to less than eight thousand. As Wade Davis recounts: "For each ton of rubber produced, ten Indians were slaughtered and hundreds left scarred for life with the welts and wounds that became known throughout the Northwest Amazon as *la marca arana,*— the mark of Arana."

There are many instances of cruel violence in the history of South America and the world, but this is certainly one of the darkest episodes.

Eventually this came to the world's attention. In 1907 a young American by the name of Walter Hardenburg began a trip, apparently solely for the adventure of it, into South America. He wanted to see the Amazon. Hardenburg and a friend named Perkins worked their way down through Central and South America. Then, heading south from Buenaventura on the Pacific coast of Colombia they entered the Rio Putumayo. Local authorities advised the pair to travel the Rio Napo as they might get into trouble going down the Rio Putumayo. Of course, this was a challenge for the two young Americans (Hardenburg was twenty-one), and, not surprisingly, they chose the Putumayo.

It proved to be a revelation. Hardenburg discovered the horrible treatment of the Indians and attempted to report it to the world. He spent years trying to get someone to listen. Much of this effort took place while he was living in Iquitos. In 1912 he wrote a book titled *Putumayo, The Devil's Paradise*. Finally, he was heard in London, England.

After an English investigation (much of the stock in Arana's company was held by the English) the Parliament's House of Lords set up a select committee. But in the end nothing was done and Arana himself went on to a distinguished career in public service. Reportedly, he became a Peruvian senator and died at age 88 in 1952.

But, despite the efforts of Hardenburg and others, the horrors of the rubber boom were brought to an end by economic and political forces, not by humanitarian actions.

In 1876, an Englishman smuggled out a large quantity of rubber tree seeds to the botanical gardens in London. From there they were transported to Asia. In just a few years Asian production, primarily in Malaysia and Ceylon (now Sri Lanka), took over the world market and the great rubber boom in the Amazon collapsed.

The rubber trees can grow in rows in Asia while they must be widely scattered in South America. This fact results from the existence of a leaf blight in South America which does not exist in Asia. Having the trees close together and not in jungles reduces the labor costs a great deal.

Another factor bringing about the end of the fuss over rubber (both the inhumane treatment of the Indians and the market) was the beginning of World War I in 1914.

The afternoon trip was a boat ride into some very beautiful small tributaries. Again, our guide showed us many interesting aspects of the rain forest including the water-hyacinth. This plant is native to Amazonia and is kept under control there by the balance of nature. However, other locales where it has been introduced, sometimes inadvertently, have not been so lucky. It has clogged waterways in several places around the world.

The jacana are amusing birds to watch. You will see many of them walking in a stiff manner on floating vegetation. These long-legged, delicately-proportioned birds are considered a marsh bird.

More sloths were sighted today as well.

Our return took us back into the Amazon where our small boat's motor died. The boat carried no means of communication and we were near the bank on the wrong side of the wide river. We were in no immediate trouble, but we weren't moving. Amid much laughter and joking one of the men in the group began rowing with a broom and the others took up loose floorboards and began paddling.

One of the women feared the boat was going to sink because the floorboards had been lifted. This was amusing to the other passengers, but I'm sure it was not funny to her.

We couldn't have made it across the Amazon but we had fun trying. After 20 or 30 minutes, the pilot got the outboard motor started after all. On our way back to the lodge, we met a boat from the lodge coming out to look for us as we were overdue. Your safety is certainly well looked after on these trips.

In the evening, we saw a tapir near the dining room. The "wild" critter apparently hangs around the dining room in hopes of scrounging some bananas. The tapir is the largest terrestial mammal in the region. It is the size of a small pony, but it looks like a combination of pig and rhinoceros.

The minor crises we experienced today are part of the fun of small group touring.

CHAPTER 10

EXPLORNAPO CAMP

*T*he morning trip from the lodge to Explornapo Camp was a pleasant hour and a half boat ride.. Swinging out into the Rio Napo we passed a monument to Francisco de Orellana, one of the early explorers of the Amazon.

There is evidence that people lived in the Amazon basin "only" 12,000 to 15,000 years ago. In contrast, humans (or pre-humans) lived in Africa many millions of years ago. Also different is the fact that waves of outsiders invaded Africa and Europe in days of antiquity, but no explorer entered the Amazon area before about the fifteenth century.

Before the Amazon was discovered, Spain and Portugal signed the Treaty of Tordesillas in 1494, dividing the unknown world between the two empires. The dividing line was a longitudinal line 350 leagues (about 1000 miles or 1600 km) west of the Cape Verde Islands. Everything undiscovered west of that line was to belong to Spain and all lands to the east would belong to Portugal. Much of what is now Brazil lies to the east of that imaginary line, which is why Brazilians speak Portuguese while most of the rest of Latin America speaks Spanish.

The jungle air is so hot and humid, its land so waterlogged, its trees and plants so full of termites and other destructive insects that very little made by man can survive for more than a few years let alone four centuries. Thus we have no relics of these early explorers:

Amerigo Vespucci (1454-1512), the man who gave his name to America was probably the first non-Indian to reach the Amazon. But he only briefly explored the mouth in the year 1499. Some writers claim that Vicente Pinzon was the first European to see the Amazon. Possibly Pinzon and Vespucci were on the same ship.

Francisco de Orellana (1511 to 1546). A Spaniard, Orellana was the first person to sail (or, rather, float) virtually the entire length of the Amazon. This was in 1542. His goal was not to explore, but to find gold and cinnamon.

Interestingly, the legend of the gold that the Indians claimed existed to the east may have been the result of a misunderstanding. The word for "gold" in the Quechua language is the word for "stone" in Tupi. The Quechua language was spoken by the Incas while the Tupi tribe lived to the east. So, it may be that the Indians reported the existence of stones (there are very few in the Amazon basin) and the Spaniards thought they were saying gold.

Earlier, Orellana served in Francisco Pizarro's army during the brutal conquest of the Incas in southern Peru. He lost an eye during the Inca campaign.

A relatively humane and intelligent man as conquistadors went, he learned the Indians' language and was primarily a diplomat, although he could be a conqueror on occasion. He operated at times under the command of the ruthless Gonzalo Pizarro.

Gonzalo Pizarro (1506[?]-1548) was the younger brother of the infamous Francisco Pizarro, conqueror of Peru and the Inca Empire. Gonzalo was appointed Governor of Quito (now capitol of Ecuador) in about 1540. He formed and led an expedition into the Amazon area but he probably never reached the river itself, while his second-in-command, Orellana, pushed on and went all the way down the Amazon to the ocean.

There is a historical controversy about Orellana's expedition. Orellana's boss, Gonzalo Pizarro, felt that his assistant had betrayed him. Pizarro contended that he had dispatched Orellana down the river for the purpose of scouting, locating food, and returning.

Orellana's chronicler, **Friar Gaspar de Carvajal**, does not mention this fact although he covers the expedition in some detail. Whether or not Orellana had defied the orders of his superior, Gonzalo Pizarro, remains a matter of dispute among historians. Anthony Smith explains this in his book, *Explorers of the Amazon*.

If Orellana was supposed to return and didn't, it may have been because of the great difficulty of paddling upstream on the Amazon. (The coming of the gasoline motor was a terrific boon to travelers on the Amazon.)

Francisco de Orellana was the one who named the Amazon because he saw (or thought he did) some large, fierce female warriors. In Greek mythology, there are tales of such women, called Amazons.

The giant river was known as the Orellana for a few years, but gradually it came to be called the Amazon.

Smith's account comes from the record kept by Orellana's friar. When the expedition was in what is today Brazil, one of the tribes they met told the explorers of a tribe of women warriors nearby. Smith says:

> Right from the outset the Spanish referred to these people as 'Amazons,' and of course one wonders why.
>
> There is a similar Indian word (in Tupi-Guarani) meaning tidal bore, also referring to those living in the affected area. A tidal bore is where an outflowing river meets the incoming tide from the ocean. The tidal bore on the Amazon is a dramatic sight as the waters roil and tumble spectacularly.
>
> To this legend is added the notion of their name deriving from a-mazos, or 'no breast.' Whether there ever were Scythian women who valiantly removed one mammary gland to improve their archery (which does not seem necessary) will never be known. What is known is that Carvajal names these South American women 'Amazons' the moment he first writes of them. No one in his party, it seems, ever called them anything else.

Some days later, the expedition came across and fought with these women warriors, shooting seven or eight. As Orellana's friar wrote:

These women are very white and tall, and have hair very long and braided and wound about the head, and they are very robust and go about naked, [but] with their privy parts covered, with their bows and arrows in their hands, doing as much as ten Indian men, and indeed there was one woman among these who shot an arrow a span deep into one of the brigantines [boats the expedition had built], and others less deep, so that our brigantines looked like porcupines.

These warrior women have never been seen since, so how much validity is there to this story?

In Greek mythology the Amazons were a nation of female warriors ruled by a queen. No man was permitted to dwell in their country, which was on the south coast of the Black Sea. Male infants were sent to their fathers, the Gargareans, in a neighboring land. The girls were trained in agriculture, hunting, and the art of war.

According to the myths, Amazons invaded Greece, Syria, the Arabian Peninsula, Egypt, Libya, and the islands of the Aegean. Legends tell of the adventures of Hercules and Theseus in the land of the Amazons.

In various parts of the globe anthropologists have found peoples among whom the rights of the mother exceed those of the father and women have an importance that elsewhere belongs to men. Such a society is called a matriarchate. Most mythology experts believe the Amazon myths arose from tales of such societies.

History records many instances of women warriors. In modern times the king of Dahomey (now Benin) had an army of women. A female so-called "battalion of death" fought in the Russian Revolution of 1917. Women soldiers served with Soviet troops in World War II. The South Korean army had women fighters in 1950. Women are active in the Israeli army.

The Yagua tribe, one of the 60 or so Indian tribes still existing in the Amazon, wears a costume that resembles a skirt. Could it be that these Yaguas are the origin of the name of this mighty river? They live near the confluence of the Napo and the Amazon; it was the Rio Napo which the Orellana expedition traversed on its way from Ecuador to the Atlantic.

One difficulty with this theory is that the women warriors Carvajal describes lived much farther downriver. However, the tribes did move from time to time.

Lope de Aguirre (1511[?]-1561) was clearly the most brutal of the early Spanish explorers. Today, we would probably call him a sociopath or psychotic and a serial killer, but even in the violent 16th century in Peru, he was considered a crazed and dangerous man.

Like Orellana, he started out on his Amazonian expedition as its second-in-command. Orellana, though, took off on his own expedition at the urging of his commander. Aguirre had his superior killed. One gains a feeling for this man's fierce cruelty from the 1972 film, *Aguirre, The Wrath of God.*

Aguirre was such a feared and hated man that after his violent death, his enemies destroyed everything they could find that was related to him. Consequently, it has been impossible for historians to trace the exact route of his expedition. Apparently, he started from Lima and went all the way to the Atlantic. He may have gone down the Amazon to the ocean. Or he may have diverged up the Rio Negro (in present-day Brazil), then followed the Orinoco through Venezuela to the Caribbean. Whichever way, he almost certainly passed through the part of the Peruvian Amazon now covered by both the Intenational Expedition trips.

A century or so later, in 1637 **Pedro Teixeira**, a Portuguese explorer, ascended the Amazon with 2,000 men in 47 canoes.

About 1751 **Charles Marie de la Condamine**, a French scientist, made the first geographical survey of the basin. When he returned to Europe, he took with him the deadly Indian arrow poison, curare. Curare's usefulness in medicine was not discovered for another century. Curare will be discussed later in this book.

An example of the dangers faced by early explorers can be found in this true account:

Though she was not an explorer, the remarkable **Isabela Godin des Odonais** lived through an incredible journey down the Amazon. In 1769, the Peruvian began a trek to join her French husband who had gone downriver twenty years before. The couple intended to leave together, but the husband apparently decided to scout the route first, then return for his wife. But he had not realized how difficult it was to paddle up river. So, unable to travel back to her, he stayed and waited for her to follow him.

For reasons not recorded, she did not attempt to join him until 20 years had passed. Then she set out, accompanied by 31 Indians, three Frenchmen, three female servants, and her faithful slave, Joachim. Also in the party were her two brothers and her 12 year-old nephew.

The party left Riobamba, in present day Ecuador. Their first stop was to be at a prosperous village downriver. When they arrived they found only smoldering remains. The village, after being decimated by a smallpox epidemic, had been put to the torch. The 31 Indians quickly disappeared into the jungle.

After some discussion, the group decided to go on. One of the Frenchmen volunteered to steer the canoe, but his hat flew off and he fell in the river in attempting to retrieve it. Once he was in the water, a floating log hit him in the head, and he was never seen again. Later that day, their canoe struck a log and dumped the remaining nine travelers into the river. They managed to scramble ashore.

For some reason one of the Frenchmen and Joachim took the canoe and traveled ahead to the next village. In this less swift-flowing part of the river, they would be able to return and were expected to in a few days. After a dozen days with no sign or word of the advance party, Mme. Godin ordered a raft built for the seven remaining travelers. No sooner had it been launched than it hit a tree, disintegrated, and dumped everyone in the river.

That night the nephew, who had been sick, died. Two of the female servants died and one wandered off, never to be seen again. Isabela's two brothers and the remaining Frenchman died also. None of the bodies were buried—no one had the strength to do the job.

Isabela, the oldest member of the expedition, was now its only survivor. For two days she remained in the camp, amid the stench of corpses rotting in the warm tropical air. The bodies must have been covered with flies. Finally, she wandered into the forest, where she meandered aimlessly for nine days before coming across two Indians who took her to civilization.

Mme. Godin's incredible survival and subsequent reuniting with her husband after twenty years of separation became the talk of the salons of Paris. Eventually this remarkable woman settled in France where she and her husband lived peacefully for nineteen more years.

We arrived at the Camp and had lunch. The facilities at Explorama Lodge and Explornapo Camp are basically similar, except the lodge's private rooms are somewhat larger and the layout of the buildings is a little different.

After lunch we visited the ReNuPeRu Ethnobotanical Garden. This was donated to ACEER by James Duke, a scientist who has taken an interest in this area after his retirement from the U.S. Department of Agriculture. A full-time employee, Antonio Montero Pisco, tends the garden, which is primarily a demonstration garden of medicinal plants. He is also a practicing shaman.

Although man has studied these native medicinal plants for centuries, what he knows about them only scratches the surface. Present efforts focus on the technical aspects of extracting the essence of the plant and converting it to a form usable by non-residents of Amazonia—in other words, the commercial pharmaceutical uses of plants. This is possibly the single most important reason for mankind to understand and preserve the Amazon.

It should be clarified that the ReNuPeRu garden, though, is operated only to benefit the local people. It is a livng lab and classroom and ACEER plans on transferring the knowledge gained to local villages so they can create "green pharmacies" of their own in their villages.

Richard Schultes (1915-), is undoubtedly the greatest scientific explorer of South America in the twentieth century. The ethnobotanist and Harvard professor explored the Amazon basin from 1941 to 1953, collecting some twenty thousand botanical specimens. Three hundred of those species were new to science; some were subsequently named for him. Considered the world's greatest authority on hallucinogenic plants, he documented much of the native shamans' knowledge.

Schultes was in the Amazonian forest when the United States entered World War II in December, 1941. He was, in effect, drafted. In November, 1942 he was called to Washington, where wartime strategists gave him an assignment to re-establish the rubber industry in South America. Until America entered the war, the vast majority of its rubber came from East Asia. But Japan had commandeered those plantations, so Asian rubber was of course not available to the U.S. Although it was kept secret at the time, and is still not widely known, the United States came very close to running out of rubber during the early 40s.

Schultes was dispatched back to the rain forest to attempt to locate rubber trees of high enough quality and in areas where they were accessible for harvest. He began his search but he came down with an infection and almost died.

Later, after trekking through an extremely difficult region of the Amazon Basin, Schultes located a good number of rubber trees near navigable rivers. He reported to Washington that, given ten thousand men, that area could produce a tremendous amount of rubber. However, there was nowhere to get ten thousand men, the trees were very widespread, and there was no way enough rubber could be produced in South America, anyway. Besides, Washington was no longer interested.

Through a combination of saving existing tires (the real reason for gasoline rationing in the U.S. during World War II), buying up and reclaiming used rubber, scrounging more rubber from various international sources, and utilizing synthetic rubber extensively, the U.S. was able to muddle through the rubber shortage and win the war anyway. But the shift in the rubber industry from South America to Asia in the early years of the twentieth century almost resulted in the Allies losing World War II.

Rubber trees still grow in the Amazon and latex is harvested in some parts of Brazil. A good "feel" for the rubber boom era can be obtained from the movie *Fitzcarraldo*. The film also paints a graphic picture of life in Iquitos around the turn of the century.

About a quarter of all prescriptions dispensed in America are compounded from substances extracted from plants. Another thirteen percent come from microorganisms and three percent from animals. According to Edward O. Wilson in his book, *The Diversity of Life,* "Fewer than 3 percent of the flowering plants of the world, about 5,000 of the 220,000 species, have been examined for alkaloids, and then in limited and haphazard fashion." Many medicines have an alkaloid base.

A few examples of conditions that can be treated by native plants include: malaria, leprosy, headaches, stomach aches, infertility, skin cuts or abrasions ... the list is almost endless. In addition to treating illnesses, plants or their roots or bark can be used to prevent conception, increase sexual drive, decrease sexual drive, or even turn gray hair to black!

There is good reason to believe that there are natural products that will prove useful in controlling HIV and cancer. The fact that there are major lethal diseases which may be conquered by Amazonian plants is reason enough to increase scientific study of the area.

Currently, extracts of a few plants from the Peruvian Amazon are being analyzed by Microbotanica, a company located in New Milford, Connecticut

Over 1400 plant species from tropical rain forests are thought to have anti-cancer properties reports *The Last Rain Forests.*

In their book, *Amazonian Ethobotanical Dictionary,* James Duke and Rodolfo Vasquez list over 1500 plants. They confess, though, that this is only about 20 percent of the flora existing in the Amazon.

Quinine, extracted from tree bark, may be the premier medicinal product of South

America. Long used in the prevention and treatment of malaria, its effectiveness proved to be time-limited. Malaria was virtually controlled by quinine, until the organism developed tolerance to it. Then we switched to chloroquinine and synthetics. Eventually, tolerance was again developed and we went back to the forest for *qing hao*. At present, the malaria bug is developing a tolerance for this, too.

This illustrates one reason it is so important to preserve the rain forest and its biodiversity. We may need to return to the forest and find another drug to deal with diseases that build up resistance to effective treatments. Also we need to constantly be on the lookout for effective treatments of new strains of diseases, or even new diseases. There are at least six natural products in the Amazon that hold promise of treating AIDS, for example.

"Preservation of biodiversity is self preservation."

James Duke and Rodolfo Vasquez

Today the rain fell hard while we napped, but by the time we were ready for the afternoon trip it was sunny again. Another gorgeous boat trip took us through a very narrow inlet into a fantastic lake. We saw many birds, including five more hoatzins and many giant water lilies.

At supper, I talked with Peter Jenson, the dynamic head of Explorama Tours, which operates Explorama Lodge and Explornapo Camp. Jenson is an American anthropologist who landed in Iquitos over thirty years ago. Fascinated by the area, as so many of us are, he proceeded to establish the business much as it is today.

The remarkable cooperation between Explorama Tours, International Expeditions,

ACEER, and CONOPAC certainly bodes well for the future preservation and study of the Amazon. Other organizations, both Peruvian and U.S. based, are involved in the efforts. Funding for these causes comes almost entirely from the fees paid by ecotourists. At the same time, these trips demonstrate to the local people that it is in their best interests to do everything they can to preserve their uniquely beautiful land.

That night in my room, after I washed my hands in the enamel washbasin, I threw the dirty water out the window, as is the custom.

But my soapy hands could not grip the washbasin very firmly. So, the washbasin went sailing out the window along with the dirty water. The hysterical laughter that this amusing accident caused was not quickly stilled.

International Expeditions by Hugh Hunter, Jr.

CHAPTER 11

ACEER

T *he morning trip was by boat, this time in the rain. More spectacular sights! In the afternoon we hiked to ACEER, some 35 minutes away. Along the way, Ari showed us some weirdly-colored frogs. The ACEER camp building is a rather primitive but well-built structure along the lines of Explorama Lodge and Explornapo Camp. The main difference being that ACEER has solar-powered lighting whereas the other two are lighted by kerosene lamps.*

The warm temperature and high humidity of the Amazon rain forest combine to make this the richest frog area in the world.

The amazing variety of strange specimens will be pointed out by your guide, particularly on the land expedition.

The poison-arrow frog is one of the best known residents of the Amazon basin. The amphibian's skin secretes a deadly poison, which deters certain animals from eating it. Indians discovered long ago that this gooey substance could be collected and spread on

the tips of hunting arrows. Monkeys, birds, and other prey can thus be killed with the poisoned arrows or darts in blow guns. This type of hunting is still used in some areas.

Poison-arrow frogs (also called poison-dart or dart-poison) and other small frogs frequently live and die high up in the trees. They dwell in the rain-fed pools of water found in the epiphytic plants, particularly the bromeliads. These pools-in-the-sky are miniature ecosystems in themselves, harboring a variety of life forms, including the larvae of mosquitoes and damselflies.

The frogs' bold coloring indicates their being poison and warns predators to leave these creatures alone. There are so many varieties that you may, as with butterflies, come across an undiscovered (or at least uncatalogued) species.

From so many different varieties comes a wide range of calls and voices, some of which sound like birds, insects, or even mammals.

Curare is another source of poisonous material used on arrows and darts for hunting. This well-known product of the Amazon is extracted from certain plants. It is a major drug used in modern medicine, not as a poison but as an ingredient in muscle relaxants and anesthetics. A rather eccentric English planter named Waterton uncovered curare's remarkable properties. Davis describes the nineteenth century occasion in the following words:

> He (Waterton) began by injecting the poison (curare) into the shoulder of a female donkey. In ten minutes the creature appeared to be dead. Waterton, being rather

accomplished with a blade, having bled himself on at least 136 occasions, made a small incision in the animal's windpipe and began to inflate its lungs with a bellows. The donkey revived. When Waterton stopped the flow of air, the creature once again succumbed. Resuming artificial respiration, he nursed the animal until the effects of the poison wore off. After two hours the donkey stood up and walked away. This treatment marked a turning point in the history of medicine. In demonstrating that curare caused death by asphyxiation and that the victim could be kept alive by artificial respiration, Waterton ... revealed how the remarkable properties of this muscle relaxant might be used therapeutically in modern medicine.

Another poison which some travelers are apprehensive about are the notorious Amazon snakes.

Contrary to popular notion, few of the common Amazon-resident snakes are poisonous. Snakes of any kind are seldom seen, except occasionally high up in the buildings of the camps on the land expedition. Even then, it's only the non-poisonous ones.

Anacondas are now rare in this part of the Amazon. Despite Hollywood's portrayal of them, the huge serpents neither bite nor crush humans.

Many other types of snakes exist in the Amazon, but are seldom seen except by herpetologists who are searching for them.

Turtles were once quite common in the area. Unfortunately, the turtles and their eggs are such excellent food that their number has dwindled so dramatically that they are seldom seen in the wild now. However, the Amazon provides an excellent environment for turtles; in fact, turtle farming on a commercial scale presents an opportunity for economic development in the area. The first Europeans to enter the Amazon found the Indians raising and utilizing large numbers of turtles, mainly for food.

Mother Nature enables some of her offspring to protect themselves by giving them the ability to assume the appearance of other species, or of their surroundings. Some insects, flora, and fauna (especially birds and flowers) can mimic other species. Some caterpillars that are not poisonous resemble those that are. Some insects seem to be twigs. You will probably see butterflies that have 'eyes' on their wings so that certain predators may be warned away. There are even fish that look like leaves!

Though this adaptation is not unique to the Amazon, it occurs much more often here than elsewhere.

Beetles constitute the largest biological order with some 300,000 known species. As with butterflies and frogs, there are some fantastic specimens to be seen.

A butterfly farm is scheduled to be established in 1999 at ACEER's main location.

Ants: According to Edward O. Wilson, one of the world's top authorities on ants, "In the Amazon rain forest they [ants] compose more than 10 percent of the biomass of all animals. This means that if you were to collect, dry out, and weigh every animal in a piece of forest, from monkeys and birds down to mites and roundworms, at least 10 percent would consist of these insects alone. Ants make up almost half of the insect biomass overall and 70 percent of the individual insects found in the treetops."

Although all ants share physical and social traits, there are many distinct varieties that differ in their habits and appearance. They are classified according to the shape of certain parts of their bodies and by specific behaviors.

Army ants are sometimes called driver ants or legionary ants. There are about 200 species. These wanderers do not build permanent nests; instead, they cling together on logs or in hollow trees. They travel in columns, sometimes at speeds of up to 65 feet (20 meters) per hour. Some of these columns reportedly contain up to 20 million ants. When a swarm of army ants marches through a human settlement, it can destroy all crops and any small animals in its path. You will probably see army ants on either trip.

Leaf-cutter ants are quite common. These industrious ants cut flowers and leaves into small pieces, then carry them overhead like green umbrellas. This earns them their alternate name, parasol ants. They engage in agriculture: leaf-cutters grow a fungus on decaying leaf pieces, carefully tend it like farmers, and harvest it for food. You will almost certainly see these fascinating insects.

Amazon ants are unable to gather food, build nests, or feed their young by themselves. They invade the nests of other species, killing the workers and bringing home the helpless young ants to raise as slaves and do the work of the colony. You may not see these ants.

Aztec ants live in cecropia trees and protect them from all predators except sloths and a few other herbivores that feed on cecropias. The symbiotic interaction between aztec ants and cecropia trees is one of the better understood relationships in Amazonia.

The process begins with birds, bats, fish, and other animals dispersing the tiny cecropia seeds. Within a year after the annual floods recede the tree is well established and thriving. The tree is soon colonized by aztec queen ants, which gain occupancy by chewing through the stem into the hollow central cavity. Like bamboo, the stems of the cecropia tree are divided into compartments. The queen passes through the thin membrane between the compartments, sealing the hole after her.

She then lays her eggs. The young hatchlings are cared for by worker ants who chew holes in the membranes and colonize the entire plant. The workers fend off intruders—including visiting animals, birds, and would-be ant queens seeking plants to colonize. The ants-in-residence feed on their host's leaves. In return for room and board, the ants groom their home tree of germinating epiphytes. The host cecropia thus outgrows its competitors; indeed, its ant occupants eliminate the competition.

The tree, in turn, provides nectar and protein for its defenders. At the points where the leaves and trunks join are tiny white capsules called Müllerian bodies. The capsules are rich in protein. Thus the cecropia furnishes all the nutrients the ants require, obviating the necessity for them to forage elsewhere—giving them more time to spend on sentry duty protecting the tree. Thus, the tree gives sustenance; the ants give protection.

As the flood levels rise during the high water period, the ants climb upward. Insect-eating fish gather, awaiting the tree's complete submersion. It is not unusual, late in the high water season, to see hordes of ants huddled on the upper leaves just before the rising water drowns them.

Many ant species have specific circumscribed areas, dividing up their world into territories. Similar to what humans do with the earth.

Termites are actually critical for the ecology of the rain forest and very beneficial in nutrient recycling. Although destructive to buildings they play an important role in the forest.

The warmth and moisture of the rain forest generate an abundance of fungi of various types. After dark, Ari invited us to step out into the forest to see a sight discovered by the ACEER staff.

Extinguishing our flashlights, we saw ... fungi plants glowing in the dark. As far as I know, these phosphorescent leaves are unknown to science.

When you visit the Amazon, perhaps you will discover a new life form.

Mary Lutz

Mary Lutz

CHAPTER 12

THE CANOPY WALKWAY

We arose early and walked the ten minutes to the Canopy Walk way. Sighting along the treetops to the horizon, yet at the same time being physically close to flora and fauna .... a beautiful, breathtaking, almost spiritual experience!

Although uncomfortable with heights myself, I found the walk so fascinating that my trepidation was almost irrelevant. For those with the same phobia, I recommend deep breathing to relax before stepping out onto the suspension bridge on the walkway.

The canopy walkway is anchored to the ground at either end. Climbing the stairs of the end tower one then accesses a suspension bridge to the next, tree-based, tower. Climbing the stairs once again one finds another suspension bridge. The tower stairways are connected by twelve suspension bridges, forming a quarter-mile walkway up through,

"The rain forest, in many ways, is like a multi-storey business building where many distinct groups of activities are concentrated on different floors, or tiers of floors, with many workers moving from one level to the next during the course of a day or night."

Michael Goulding

then above, the canopy of the forest. Both tourists and scientists use the walkway; indeed, that is where scientists conduct much of the observation on which they base their research.

The suspensions consist of V-shaped netting with aluminum ladders topped by wooden planks along the bottom. The netting is secured to cables that serve as handrails. Net-and-cable form a waist-to-shoulder-high enclosure, so that walkers are safe and secure.

Each solidly constructed segment of walkway is firmly fastened by cables to large trees. Wooden insulators protect the trunks from being gouged by the cables.

The towers are constructed around trees, except for the ones at each end, which are based on eight poles embedded in the ground. The walkway can be traversed in either direction.

There are safety rules for crossing the walkway. No more than four people on a platform at once. No more than three people on any one suspension at a time. Walkers are urged not to have insect repellent on their hands as the chemicals tend to deteriorate the ropes of the netting.

Limiting the numbers results in some delays when several people are on the walkway at once. But then, it gives you an opportunity to enjoy the rain forest from above. The walkway, rising to a height of about 120 feet, is continually maintained by trained experts. As a matter of fact, it is inspected twice a day.

From the walkway, the view of the forest canopy extends as far as the eye can see. This is a dramatic sight, particularly at sunrise or sunset. From here, tourist and scientist alike gain a close-up observation of forest activity, and of the birds, flowers, animals, epiphytes and thousands of other organisms existing there in abundance.

Returning to the walkway in the afternoon, we saw several baby Saki monkeys watching us from not 20 feet (6 m) off the walkway.

The saki monkey (*Monk Saki Monkey*) has a body length of 17 inches (43 cm), with the tail a bit longer. Sakis are dark, except for an almost bald crown and nearly naked face. Relatively quiet animals, they call with low-pitched whines, grunts, and chirps. They usually travel in groups of three or four and tend to live in the middle to upper parts of the forest. Sakis were seen on 73 percent of the 1996 voyages.

Some scientists say that there are distinct levels to the rain forest, but Nalini M. Nadkarni, President of the International Canopy Network, says there are lots of exceptions to this idea, making it a meaningless concept.

Perhaps half of all life on earth exists in the canopy of the rain forests—forms and classes and species of epiphytes, mosses, lichens, insects, mammals, birds, and reptiles; the number is astounding.

Different species inhabit different levels—or multiple levels: Some move to different levels at different times of the day or year. The incredible variety of life leads some to call a rain forest canopy "the last unexplored frontier on earth."

The canopy of the rain forest compares to the outer edges of a coral reef in that both fringe their ecosystem. Biologists estimate that about eighty percent of the food in a forest is produced in the canopy.

Scientists and explorers have long yearned to get up to the treetops to observe what is there. Sir Francis Drake is thought to be the first non-native to climb a giant tree in a rain forest. As you may remember from your history classes, in 1537 he climbed a tree in Panama and saw the Pacific Ocean to his left and the Atlantic to the right. Supposedly, his idea of circumnavigating the globe was born in that treetop.

Over the next several centuries scientists made various attempts to learn more about the Amazon canopy. They dispatched Indians to gather specimens of particular lifeforms. Researchers trained monkeys to retrieve fruits from the treetops, but the the animals tended to eat their assignments rather than turn them in for scientific study. Trees were felled but few animals survived the fall; those that did fled into the jungle. Guns were sometimes used to shoot animals and birds ... but that left the men of science with dead subjects.

Finally, in 1929, Major Hingston led an expedition into British Guiana, where the explorers tried a different approach to putting man into the canopy. With true military thoroughness, Major Hingston assaulted the canopy with an arsenal of rocket-firing apparatus, line-throwing guns, rope ladders, parachute slings borrowed from the RAF, scaling ladders, and safety belts. Spray syringes were also on hand, as the expedition expected to be assaulted, themselves ... by noxious insects.

Despite some difficulties (which all explorations encounter), the expedition was quite successful.

Over the years, man has devised various approaches to enable himself to peer into the canopy, thus both satisfying his curiosity and adding to his scientific knowledge. These "approaches" included ladders, cranes, block & tackle systems, a bosun's chair, and even a dirigible.

Then, in the 1960s, the first canopy walkway was built in the rain forests of Malaysia. It was designed by U.S. Army Engineers.

A few other canopy walkways have been built in Asia, Africa, and Central America, but South America's only one was built by a consortium consisting of International Expeditions, Explorama Tours, and the Peruvian organization CONOPAC.

ACEER then came into being to, among other programs, operate the Canopy Walkway.

How ACEER came about is a story in itself. It was Dr. Richard Ryel, President of International Expeditions, who first proposed the walkway...and conceptualized ACEER. The organization became a reality shortly after the First International Rainforest Workshop, held in Peru in 1991. The first project of the newly formed non-profit group was to build a living facility in the Amazon rain forest. This proved to be relatively easy due to the experience and expertise of the Explorama staff.

Headed by Peter Jenson, Explorama Tours has been providing a jungle experience to tourists since 1964. Explorama Lodge was built in 1964 and Explornapo Camp some years later. Over the years, the facilities have hosted many scientists and even more tourists.

Constructing the canopy walkway was another matter entirely. It took between two and three years to build this, the largest canopy walkway in the world. The primary designer or architect was Dr. Illar Muul. Previously, Dr. Muul built such walkways in Malaysia and China.

Acquisition of the materials was complicated. Special aluminum ladders were imported from Malaysia. Steel cable, ropes, safety netting, and hardware came from various places in the U.S. The ladders were shipped by mistake to New York and a truck had to be hired to bring them to Miami.

Faucett Airlines then flew the ladders and the other equipment to Iquitos. From there they were hand-carried to boats, then transported to the Rio Napo landing, from there they were again hand-carried to the walkway site.

It is thought to be the only environmental project of this magnitude which was funded primarily with tourist dollars.

Many people, both Americans and Peruvians, were involved in this project. Two American ornithologists, Paul Donahue and Teresa Wood, moved to Peru for a year and supervised the day-to-day engineering and trained the Peruvian walkway builders and inspectors.

The ACEER has many other projects, both present and planned for the future, in addition to the canopy walkway. They are involved in the development of Geographic Information System (GIS), satellite technology

"To reach into the rain forest roof is not an easy task either for man or for the giant trees."

Andrew W. Mitchell

studying the various ecosystems in this part of the rain forest. In addition, they have recently completed a conservation study of the Rio Tapiche watershed, and conduct workshops for Peruvian scientists, a pharmacist's workshop, an educational workshop for American teachers, a children's rain forest workshop, Peruvian teacher training, an Adopt-a-School program, a community garden building project, and a community library project.

ACEER is also involved in pollution control and abatement projects for the city of Iquitos, helping people learn how to handle the oil spills which occasionally occur at the oil facilities. They are developing a CD-ROM software program about the rain forest. ACEER is not planning to expand geographically but they will be expanding programmatically. About one-half of the funds which support the foundation now come from tourists.

Scientifically, the canopy walkway has already resulted in the discovery of a new species of lizard and much new information about bromeliads.

Roger Mustalish, the President of ACEER, is on the faculty of West Chester University in Pennsylvania. He gives an interesting account of how he became affiliated with the Center. Dr. Mustalish was Acting Dean of the university's School of Health Sciences at the university when the school's president asked him to become permanent Dean. Dr. Mustalish accepted the promotion, but said he would complete the necessary paperwork after he returned from vacation. His vacation was to the Amazon and, specifically, to ACEER. The canopy walkway was already in existence and he found himself enthralled by the project.

Upon his return to the United States, Dr. Mustalish flew to the headquarters of International Expeditions near Birmingham, Alabama. After talking with Dr. Richard Ryel (the President of International Expeditions who came up with the idea for both the canopy walkway and ACEER and was its first President), Roger Mustalish became further enamored with the project. Soon, he took over the presidential reins himself. He never did become a dean at West Chester University.

ACEER receives a per-passenger contribution from International Expeditions. In order to contribute directly to ACEER, see the donor information in the back of this book.

The rain made the trails wetter and the rivers higher. Not good for trekking the forest. We boated back to Explornapo Camp for a brief stop, then returned to Explorama Lodge.

Our group was relaxed and laughing more today as the end of our odyssey approached.

To see an example of a small factory along the Amazon, our guides walked us from the lodge to a nearby rum distillery. At the site was the factory, a small farm (where the owner kept water buffalo), and a general store. North Americans may think the facility a little primitive, but the ribereños operated the enterprise efficiently. Some in the group sampled the factory's product.

Ari, our guide, presented a very interesting talk on Indian culture, and we followed it up with an afternoon visit to a Yagua Indian village. The villagers had prepared an exhibit of handcrafted items for sale, all arranged in a big circle. It reminded me of a fair in a small town, but the

*person in the middle of the circle made it differ-
ent. He was wearing a skirt and demonstrating
the use of a blowgun.*

*That evening, our last, Ari's band performed
in the gift shop/lounge at Explorama Lodge—a
relaxing, jungle-setting version of a night club!*

Mary Lutz

It has been demonstrated that plant products in the Peruvian Amazon are potentially
more profitable in the long run than the traditional logging. Also, ecotourism is rapidly
becoming an important source of income for
individuals living in those wild areas.

Only in recent years have economists be-
gun to realize the economic potential of all
the products of the rain forest. This is hardly
a new idea to the people who have lived there
for thousands of years. In its economic study
of a section of the Amazon forest, the Insti-
tute of Economic Botany estimated that fruits
and latex represent more than 90 percent of

the total market value of products in that section. Also, of course, the harvesting of nuts, fruits, and rubber does much less damage to the forests than the harvesting of trees.

Even treetop products such as orchids, medicinal products, and edible species have been considered for their economic potential.

The emphasis on timber as the most valued commercial product of the forests may be due to the fact that it is more easily sold for hard currency and thus is of more interest to the governments of underdeveloped countries. The selling of fruits in village markets can be very important to local people, but it is almost invisible to governments.

Another theory for the bias toward logging as the main source of revenue from a forest is that business and governmental persons from Europe and the United States do not understand the qualitative differences between temperate and tropical forests. In Europe and the U.S., forests have little commercial value beyond their timber (and minerals in some areas). Tropical forests have many resources other than lumber.

As is said in THE LAST RAIN FORESTS, "Overlooking the non-wood products may be a case of the application of Western thinking and techniques to tropical forests in inappropriate ways."

It has been estimated that tropical rain forests contain more than 50 percent of the world's genetic material. This alone is an overwhelming reason for retaining and preserving the rain forests of the world.

Your trip to the Peruvian Amazon will help save it. The financial contribution you make when signing on to the river voyage and/or the land expedition will assist both the local people and scientists. Scientists are convinced that the cornucopia that is the rain forest has just barely been tapped.

In addition, you will have one of the most rewarding experiences of your life. The beauty and fascination of life in the rain forest is virtually without equal on this earth. And the 'HIDDEN AMAZON' may be the most accessible, yet pristine, rain forest to be found.

GO THERE!

BIBLIOGRAPHY

Books

Beaver, Milly Sangama de and Paul. *Tales of the Peruvian Amazon*. Largo, Fla., AE Publications, 1989.

> A rather informal compilation of legends and stories of the natives of this area.

Collier, Richard. *The River that God Forgot: The Story of the Amazon Rubber Boom*. London, Collins, 1968.

> A vivid account of the boom that decimated the Indians of the Amazon.

Collins, Mark, Editor. *The Last Rain Forests, A World Conservation Atlas*. Foreword by David Attenborough, New York, Oxford University Press, 1990.

> A beautiful, coffee-table book with excellent maps and photos. Describes features of the rain forests of the world, not only the Amazon. This book contains many scientific facts.

Cousteau, Jacques-Yves. *Jacques Cousteau's Amazon Journey*. New York, Harry N. Abrams, Inc., 1984.

> Another large-format book with stunning photographs. An account of Cousteau's trip up the Amazon.

Davis, Wade. *One River: Exploration and Discoveries in the Amazon Rain Forest*. New York, Simon & Schuster, 1996.

> An interesting book that is both a biography of the great botanist, Richard Schultes, and an account of the author's adventures traveling and plant collecting in South America.

Denslow, Julie Sloan and Christine Padoch. *People of the Tropical Rain Forest*. Berkeley-Los Angeles-London, University of California Press, 1988.

A large-format paperback consisting of several professional contributions assembled by the Smithsonian Institution.

Duke, James Alan and Rodolfo Vasquez. *Amazonian Ethnobotanical Dictionary*. Boca Raton, Florida, CRC Press, 1994.

A detailed analysis of over 1500 plants of the Peruvian Amazon with a review of the conditions they are used to treat.

Duplaix, Nicole and Noel Simon. *World Guide to Mammals*. New York, Greenwich House, 1983.

A layman's description of every mammal in the world.

Eisenberg, John F. *Mammals of the Neotropics, The Northern Neotropics, Volume I*. Chicago, University of Chicago Press, 1989.

A scientific description of the mammals of northern South America.

Emmons, Louise H. *Neotropical Rainforest Mammals, A Field Guide*. Chicago, University of Chicago Press, 1990.

Detailed scientific information for those wanting to know more about the animals of the rain forest.

Eu, Geoffrey, Editor. *Amazon Wildlife (INSIGHT GUIDE)*. Boston, Houghton Mifflin, 1995.

As with most books on the Amazon, the Peruvian part of the Amazon gets short shrift, but this is a good review of the Amazon nevertheless.

Furneaux, Robin. *The Amazon: The Story of a Great River.* New York, G. P. Putnam's Sons, 1970. (First published in Great Britain by Hamish Hamilton Ltd.)

This excellent work was the source of much of the information in this book. Contains historical facts this author didn't find elsewhere.

Gentry, Dr. Alwyn. *Preliminary Survey of the Bushmaster Trail.* mimeographed by Explorama Lodge, October, 1980.

This describes a number of plants that were kept in the garden at Explorama Lodge.

Goodman, Susan E. *Bats, Bugs, and Biodiversity: Adventures in the Amazonian Rain Forest.* Photographs by Michael J. Doolittle, New York, Atheneum, 1995.

Although packaged as a children's book, this book presents many photos and details about the 'land expedition' described in HIDDEN AMAZON.

Goulding, Michael. *Amazon: The Flooded Forest.* New York, Sterling Publishing Company, 1990. (First published in Great Britain by BBC Books).

Written to complement a British television series, this is an excellent review of the science of the Amazon.

Hardenburg, W.E. *The Putumayo, The Devil's Paradise.* London, T. Fisher Unwin, 1912.

The classic work that exposed the abuses of the rubber trade in the Amazon.

Hilty, Steven L. and William L. Brown. *A Guide to the Birds of Colombia.* Princeton, New Jersey, Princeton University Press, 1986.

Describing birds in an area quite close to the Peruvian Amazon, this is a valuable reference for serious birders.

Kane, Joe. *Running the Amazon*. New York, Vintage Books, 1989.

A fascinating account of kayaking the entire length of the Amazon. The author, understandably, focuses on the hardships rather than on the beauties of the 'River Sea'.

Keatinge, Richard W. *Peruvian Prehistory: An overview of pre-Inca and Inca society*. Cambridge, England, Cambridge University Press, 1988.

Although dealing mainly with Inca society, this book of cultural anthropology contains a section on the rainforest written by J. Scott Raymond.

Kricher, John C. *A Neotropical Companion: An Introduction to the Animals, Plants, and Ecosystems of the New World Tropics*. Princeton, New Jersey, Princeton University Press, 1989.

An excellent book on the South and Central American rain forests.

Lathrap, Donald W. *The Upper Amazon*. United Kingdom, Thames and Hudson, 1970.

A detailed scientific analysis of the early Indan cultures of a large area of the Amazon Basin. Includes considerable archeological information.

McConnell, Rosemary. *The Amazon*. Morristown, New Jersey, Silver Burdett Company, 1978.

One of the *Rivers of the World* series, this is a very clear description of the river, focusing mostly on Brazil.

Meggers, Betty J. *Amazonia: Man and Culture in a Counterfeit Paradise*. Chicago, Illinois, Aldine-Atherton, Inc., 1971.

A scientific review, emphasizing anthropology, of the development of the Amazon. As is true of virtually every book in this bibliography, the focus is on the Brazilian Amazon, not the Peruvian section.

Minta, Stephen. *Aguirre*. New York, Henry Holt and Company, 1994.

A well-told account of the Spanish Conquistador's insane journey to the sea. The author retraced Aguirre's travels and reveals much about modern Peru. Also a good account of the great rubber boom.

Mitchell, Andrew. W. *The Enchanted Canopy*. New York, Macmillan, 1986.

Contains a wealth of information about life in the rainforests of the world. Also has a great deal of information about the cooperation between species.

Moffett, Mark W. *The High Frontier: Exploring the Tropical Rainforest Canopy*. Cambridge, Massachusetts, Harvard University Press, 1993.

An excellent review of life in the rainforest canopy, especially epiphytes, insects, and the like.

Perrottet, Tony. *Peru (INSIGHT GUIDES)*. Second Edition, Boston, Massachusetts, Houghton Mifflin, 1996.

One of the most useful of the guidebooks to Peru. It includes an interesting description of the Amazon.

Perry, Donald. *Life Above the Jungle Floor*. New York, Simon & Schuster, 1986.

Although mainly about Costa Rica, this contains some interesting detail about the rain forest and describes a 'canopy web' designed by the author.

Prance, Ghillean T., and Thomas E. Lovejoy, Editors. *Amazonia*. Oxford, England, Pergamon Press, 1984.

A scientific anthology of various aspects of the Amazon.

Schmink, Marianne and Charles Wood, Editors. *Frontier Expansion in Amazonia*. Gainesville, Florida, University of Florida Press, 1984 (particularly Stocks, Anthony's paper on *Indian Policy in Eastern Peru*).

Again, most of this thoughtful book deals with Brazil, but it does contain some interesting analyses of the history of the area.

Schultes, Richard Evans and Robert F. Raffauf. *The Healing Forest: Medicinal and Toxic Plants of the Northwest Amazonia*. Portland, Oregon, Dioscorides Press (an imprint of Timber Press, Inc.), 1990.

A very thorough detailing of the medicinal plants that are known.

Smith, Anthony. *Explorers of the Amazon*. Chicago and London, University of Chicago Press, 1994.

Scholarly, but very readable account of Orellana, Aguirre, von Humboldt, and a half-dozen other early explorers of the Amazon.

Smith, Linda, M.D. *La Doctora*. Duluth, Minnesota, Pfeifer-Hamilton, 1999.

The Amazonian doctor's account of her life there.

Smith, Nigel J.H. *Man, Fishes, and the Amazon*. New York, Columbia University Press, 1981.

Although not directly quoted from in this work, this book is included in the Bibliography because it contains a wealth of information that will interest people who like fishing.

Wallace, Alfred Russel. *A Narrative of Travels on the Amazon and Rio Negro*. 1889. Second Edition, New York, Dover Publications, 1972.

Although this classic work is not about the Peruvian Amazon, it describes the rain forest as it was a century ago.

Wilson, Edward O. *The Diversity of Life*. Cambridge, Massachusetts, The Belknap Press of Harvard University Press, 1992.

Written by an outstanding scientist and writer (he has won the Pulitzer Prize twice) this book is a scientific, but very readable, examination of how the living world became diverse and how humans are destroying that diversity.

Magazine Articles

Huyghe, Patrick. "Incident at Curuça." *The Sciences*, March-April, 1996, pp. 14-17.

This article describes the meteor that struck the Amazon jungle in 1930.

McIntyre, Loren. "Consider the Source." *South American Explorer*, May, 1991, Number 29, pp. 5-14.

An account of the discovery of the source of the Amazon and a review of earlier attempts to locate it.

McIntyre, Loren. "The Amazon—Mightiest of Rivers." *National Geographic Magazine*, October, 1972, pp.445-494.

Written by the man who discovered the source of the Amazon, this is a good review of the whole river.

Movies

Herzog, Werner, Producer, *Aguirre, The Wrath of God*, (German, with English subtitles), 1972.

A retelling of the Aguirre-led expedition in the sixteenth century. Graphically portrays the horrors of this era.

Herzog, Werner, Producer, *Fitzcarraldo*, (German, with English subtitles), 1982.

The dramatization of an entrepreuner during rubber boom days in Iquitos and his quest to open up a new area for rubber production by having Indians drag his riverboat over a ridge separating two rivers.

INDEX

144

146

DONATION INFORMATION - ACEER

Name _____

Address _____

City/State/Zip _____

Phone (H) _____(W) _____

E-mail _____

Enclosed is a total of $ _____ as my contribution to support the ACEER Foundation.

The ACEER Foundation is exempt from Federal Income Tax under Section 501(c) of the Internal Revenue Code as an organization in Section 501 (c) (3).

Please make checks payable to the ACEER Foundation and mail to:

ACEER Foundation • Ten Environs Park • Helena, Alabama 35080

Phone: 205-428-1700, Ext. 242
FAX: 205-428-1714
E-mail: aceer@ietravel.com
Web site: http://orser13.erri.psu/aceer.htm

ORDER FORM - INTERNATIONAL EXPEDITIONS

Name _____

Address _____

City/State/Zip _____

Phone (H) _____(W) _____

❑ I want information about the two trips described in this book

❑ I want information about the many other trips conducted by International Expeditions.

INTERNATIONAL EXPEDITIONS

One Environs Park

Helena, Alabama 35080

or

Call 800-633-4734

or FAX 205-428-1714

ORDER FORM - DIMI PRESS

Name _____

Address _____

City/State/Zip _____

Phone _____

Enclosed is my check for $20.45 [$16.95 for *HIDDEN AMAZON* and $3.50 for shipping] or:

Credit card #: _____
   (Visa,MC, or American Express accepted)

Expiration date: _____

DIMI PRESS
3820 Oak Hollow Lane, SE
Salem, OR 97302-4774

Phone 1-800-644-DIMI(3464) for orders
or 1-503-364-7698 for further information
or FAX to 1-503-364-9727
or by INTERNET to dickbook@aol.com

Call toll-free and order now!

OTHER DIMI PRESS BOOKS FOR YOU

KOMODO, THE LIVING DRAGON (Revised Edition) by Dick Lutz & J. Marie Lutz is the only book on the world's largest lizard that is written for the non-scientist...$16.95

ALL ABOUT YOUR CAR by David Kline & Jamie Robertson is about how a car works, how to maintain it, how to buy a car, and more....$16.95

DRUGS and KIDS, How Parents Can Keep Them Apart by Gary Somdahl is a book of advice to parents on how to deal with their children when they are suspected, or proven, to be using drugs......................$14.95

WRESTLING BACK by Caren Topliff is a true account of an athlete and his mother struggling to recover from his devastating spinal cord in-jury...$14.95

HOW TO FIND THOSE HIDDEN JOBS by Violet Cooper helps job-seekers or career-changers in their search................................$13.95

SABOTAGE FLIGHT by Paul Meyerhoff II is an exciting mystery-adven-ture story for Young Adults about aviation in Alaska...........................$9.95

BRING ME A MEMORY by Rose Blue is a touching story of an 11-yr.-old girl who loses her father...$9.95

BLACK GLASS by Stuart Edelson is a novel about a gay young man coming of age in 1965 Vietnam..$19.95

DISAPPEARING ACT by Cynthia Wall is about two young people and their ham radio foiling a kidnap attempt on a cruise ship....................$5.95

A SPARK TO THE PAST by Cynthia Wall is about two young people and their ham radio accidentally being transported in time to the Oregon Trail..$6.95

Details of these books available at our web site:

http://members.aol.com/dicklutz/dimi_press.html